GOD
PLAYS
PIANO,
TOO

BRETT WEBB-MITCHELL

GOD PLAYS PIANO, TOO

The Spiritual Lives
of Disabled Children

CROSSROAD · NEW YORK

1993
The Crossroad Publishing Company
370 Lexington Avenue, New York, NY 10017
Copyright © 1993 by Brett Webb-Mitchell
Printed in the United States of America

Library of Congress Cataloging-in-Publication Data

Webb-Mitchell, Brett.
    God plays piano, too : the spiritual lives of disabled children /
Brett Webb-Mitchell.
        p. cm.
    ISBN 0-8245-1374-6
    1. Church work with mentally handicapped children. 2. Mentally
handicapped children—Religious life. 3. Spiritual life—
Christianity. I. Title.
BV4461.W43 1993
259'.4—dc20   93-21647
                                                                  CIP

Contents

Acknowledgments

The author and publisher are grateful to the following for permission to reprint:

New Oxford Review for "God Plays Piano, Too," reprinted from Volume 58, Number 5, June 1992.

Religious Education for "Listen and Learn From Narratives That Tell A Story," reprinted from Volume 85, Fall 1990.

New Oxford Review for "Opening Windows," reprinted from Volume 58, Number 1, January/February 1991.

New Oxford Review for "The Prophetic Voice of Parents with Children with Disabilities," reprinted from Volume 59, Number 10, December 1992.

Journal for Preachers for "Welcoming Unexpected Guests to the Banquet," reprinted from Volume 16, Number 3, Easter 1993.

Theology Today for "Pilgrims Lost in an Alien Land," reprinted from Volume 49, Number 3, October 1992.

New Oxford Review for "Turning the Other Cheek?," reprinted Volume 60, Number 6, July–August 1993.

Religious Education for "The Religious Imagination of Children with Disabilities," reprinted from Volume 88, Number 2, Spring 1993.

Preface

This book began when I was a doctoral student in special education at the University of North Carolina-Chapel Hill. I had been visiting Gene, a young artist in his twenties, who also happened to have mental retardation. At the time, he was living in an institution in western North Carolina. Gene already had quite a reputation in the state and region for his artwork which was evocative and thrilling to behold. Gene and I would get together once every two weeks to talk, write, and sing about God, Jesus Christ, and the Holy Spirit, for I was interested in the religious imagination of people whom society had labeled "mentally retarded." This project quickly went from being merely an intellectual enterprise to a fuller, personal dialogue between two Christians who loved the Lord. The transforming moments with Gene are captured in the chapter "Opening Windows."

These life-changing experiences, which became the articles comprising this book, have continued to push me to look and listen for, and expect to find, the surprising presence of the Holy in the lives of people whom society has deemed "disabled," and therefore *unable* to live in Christ. What made these encounters with God so surprising in the lives of those labeled "disabled" is that I found many of these people living in the most unholy kinds of places.

Going to these places, meeting these fellow Christians and friends who were Jewish, and sharing these experiences firsthand has not been a solo quest. I have been blessed by the company of family and friends who have been there for me when I had little energy, courage, or even financial resources to go on. Pam, my wife, and our children, Adrianne and Parker, have been constant companions on a journey that has led us to the most amazing places: from living in the sedate college town of Chapel Hill; studying and experiencing the richness of life in a l'Arche community in London, England; trekking across America to live in Spokane, Washington, where I continued to find stories of God in the lives of fascinating people; to Florida and my relationship with children and adolescents with behavioral, emotional, and developmental disabilities, who are the neediest of the needy, we have met God in the goodness of new friends and old acquaintances. Pam has been there to listen to and read about the stories, to share in opening the champagne in my moments of joy, and to comfort me in the stressful periods in the myriad places we have lived. In working with children with disabilities, the presence of Adrianne and Parker remind me daily of what matters in life as they are truly God's gift to our life together.

Surrounding me have been a most blessed host of people who have read and reread many of these stories, listened patiently to my phone calls as I told them of my latest encounter with God, and sharing their joy as well as their concern with the spiritual or religious wants and needs of all God's children. Dr. Stanley Hauerwas of Duke Divinity School and Dr. Jim Paul of the University of South Florida have read or heard all these stories and articles, and have been present with me throughout it all, especially when I was ready to flee from the pain of life that many children came to me with. Their constant interest in my work, care for my life, and their words of support and encouragement are truly invaluable.

Dr. George Noblit of the University of North Carolina-Chapel Hill and Dr. John Westerhoff of Duke Divinity School helped me with the ethnographic method used in collecting many of these stories. They reminded me of the integrity of the ethnographic method, and listened well to many other ethnographic projects that are still on the drawing board or ready to be implemented.

Many of these stories are from my work at Devereux Hospital and Children's Center of Florida. Dr. James and Ms. Helen Gettemy, MSW, were responsible for recruiting me from Spokane to Melbourne, Florida. Their faith in my gifts and talents with these children helped in the overall work of the Religious Narrative Project and the establishment of the Religious Life Program. Whenever life was too anxious with administrative responsibilities, Helen would always tell me to "go out and be with the children, they love you so." These were the right words at the right moment, for soon I had life back in perspective, and could carry on.

There was a core of people, professionals, paraprofessionals, and the support staff, too many to name individually, who were continually supportive of my attempt to think theologically and philosophically about the issues raised merely by the presence of these disabled children in our care. Their supportive cheers and pats on the back as I walked onto a unit or into their office, sympathizing or laughing with me, was the antidote I needed to do my work with the children.

I want to thank Jim Hanink and Dale Vree of the *New Oxford Review* who began to publish these stories and encouraged me to lean in and listen hard to what the children were trying to communicate about the mystery of God. And I thank Mike Leach of the Crossroad Publishing Company, whose excitement about these stories gave me hope that others would be interested in them as well.

Finally, I dedicate this book to the glory of God, whose presence I more fully experienced in the lives of the children and adults who trusted me enough to share their stories with me. They have taught me more about the Christian faith, and the undying love of God, in ways so concrete that even I could understand what they were trying to tell me about God's love.

Introduction
A Journey of Seeing

The introduction to this book is being written during the season of Advent. I am standing with guitar in hand at the front hall of the campus school entrance, which is buzzing with children and adolescents trying to squeeze into a too tight, hot, confining space. They gathered here tonight because it is the fourth night of Advent: we are preparing as a community for the birth of the Christ child.

We began this celebration of Advent three weeks earlier with only ten children attending worship out of 112 children living at Devereux Hospital and Children's Center of Florida. Tonight, there were forty children and adolescents, and even more direct care staff in attendance. I left the door open so that the cool evening's breeze of a Florida winter could blow in and refresh this young congregation.

We sang Christmas carols throughout the evening, opening with the traditional, exultant "Joy to the World," and ending with a raucous chorus of "Angels We Have Heard on High!" (Few children can resist getting laughingly lost in singing "Gloria.") In lighting the fourth candle this evening, otherwise known as the angels' candle, I read aloud the story of the Angel Gabriel telling Mary news of what was about to happen in her ordinary life (Luke 1:26–38). To emphasize the prominence of God's angels during this season, I retold the story of *The Littlest Angel*. It was amazing to watch these children who were trying to get comfortable on the carpeted floor at the beginning of the story, soon still, become silent and attend to this simple story of the littlest angel and his personal gift to the Christ child. The only children moving around on the floor were doing so in order to get a better look at the colorful illustrations in the book. At the end of the story, everyone was given a piece of Jesus' birthday cake. (The cake had "Happy Birthday, Jesus" on it.) After enjoying a taste of the sweet cake and the sweeter cup of hot chocolate with marshmallows on top, the children left the crowded hallway, smiling and laughing, some hugging each other, wishing one another a merry Christmas.

Later in the evening as I read and reread the description of this scene, there probably is nothing unique or unusual about this particular gathering during Advent. However, what was moving about this evening's worship was the very nature of the children gathered together: all these young people have been labeled and categorized by some authority in the health service field as having either an emotional, behavioral, or developmental disability that was severe enough that they had been taken out of their homes, their schools, their neighborhoods, and their churches, mosques, and synagogues. Suddenly, they are placed either by a state-funded human service department or their parents with private insurance money if they are lucky, into this private, nonprofit hospital of "the last hope," as some of the staff call it. It is the "last hope" for the majority of other children here who did not do well in similar, less restrictive, settings. However, what I saw before me this evening was not a congregation of children with disabilities, handicaps, limitations, and impairments. Instead, they were a gathering of talented, gifted, resilient young children and older adolescents, people whose experiences and perceptions of life and love, God and Jesus, are unique, to say the least. They have so much to contribute, along with other people in the world. I suddenly realize that we will all be the poorer and deprived of their invaluable, insightful experiences if they do not get a chance to share their God given-gifts, abilities, and talents with others.

In being sure that their story will be heard and understood, and their contributions to this life will not be rejected or ignored, I have collected their stories, and retell them in this book. Coming to the place where I can begin to hear, reflect, take into my soul, and appreciate the authentic anger and abundant joy for life shared by these young people has been a journey. They are human beings and not the "disabled other," "the handicapped," reduced to "them," and treated as an "it." Getting to this point of encountering the person with his or her unique combination of abilities and limitations has been part of a longer journey of seeing; of envisioning anew the human condition.

This journey of seeing anew is like a river. It was the writer Norman Maclean, who wrote many of his stories about rivers, canyons, and the western parts of America, like the novella, *A River Runs Through It*, who understood that stories are like a journey on a river: "I knew a story had begun, perhaps long ago near the sound of water. And I sensed that ahead I would meet something that would never erode so there would be a sharp turn, deep circles, a deposit, and quietness."[1]

Like A River

The narratives and essays collected in this book are part of a longer journey that is like a river. There are unexpected sharp turns, deep circles of quiet waters, a deposit here and there, quietness, and sometimes rough white-water rapids. Like other narrative journeys, there is a beginning, a middle, and supposedly an end. In between there are places where events come at the sojourner fast and furiously, and little is understood. At other times, things are still, if not stagnant, with lessons to be learned and shared at all times with others. Often, there are wild bends in the journey that have made my hair stand on end, as well as long, straight, narrow sections of the river journey with only the light on the horizon in sight. Sometimes the journey continues in the community of other sojourners, while at other times it is only the dim memory of the same company that upholds this traveler.

The point of departure on this journey was Beaverton High School in Oregon. During my junior year, the social studies teacher took a group of students to the soup kitchen on Burnside Street in Portland, better known as "Skid Row." At this soup kitchen I sat down and talked to people with either mental illness or mental retardation. I was engrossed by the stories they told of solitary life on the rail lines in the Pacific northwest, their tortured tour of Viet Nam during the war, or the challenge of understanding what someone was saying who had never had speech therapy and was functionally illiterate. Memory of this time stands out because these people were different from those in the suburban, upper middle-class home in which I was raised.

From there, the journey of seeing continued along the normal path expected by my parents and the school I attended. I went to Whitworth College in 1973, where I was comfortably sheltered from the "outside" world behind what was called the "pine cone curtain." I went with a love of music, a small piano scholarship, and no idea of what else I wanted to do in life. In taking the necessary, required courses, I found myself drawn to music and the psychology classes. Love of music and interest in what makes people do what they do found a common ground in the discipline of music therapy. During the January term of 1974 I began volunteer work with a music therapist at Kirbyhaven, a household of thirty men and women of all ages who were mentally retarded. I enjoyed singing with and playing piano for these new friends. When the music therapist abruptly quit her job in the fall of 1974, I was hired as the recreation therapist while still attending school. I was hooked on music therapy and work with these men and women.

With this interest in music therapy, my journey of seeing continued to the University of Kansas, where I majored in music therapy. In special education, psychology, and music therapy classes, my vision of people with disabilities was shaped and often narrowed by the social scientific perspective of disabling conditions. I began to see people with disabilities by their limitations and labels, someone to be worked *on*, to do something *to* or *for*, rather than as a person to be in relationship *with*. People became a mind-body phenomenon, with no mention of "spirit" or "faith" in the discipline of music therapy.

One invaluable piece of advice I received during this time as an undergraduate came in one of my psychology classes when the professor told my class that while we may have the best grades and college backgrounds money could buy, what was most important in doing the best job possible was our hands-on experience. With that advice, I tried to maintain a balance between my courses and experience in a worksite. During my three years in Kansas, I often had two internship sites in a semester, either working with children with mental retardation, physical impairments, or behavioral disabilities, or working at a nursing home with a group of senior citizens. These are the people who taught me what it meant to be a music therapist.

The next resting place on this journey found me completing my music therapy internship in 1978. In September of that year I began my job as a music therapist at a small school administered by the Indian River School District on the grounds of the then Hospital for the Mentally Retarded in Georgetown, Delaware. For two years I worked with children, who were severely or profoundly mentally retarded and multiply disabled, and their families, witnessing firsthand the power of music with disabled people.

One of the sudden bends in the journey of seeing that raised some important questions later in life occurred at this hospital. First, I witnessed the conscious exclusion of people with mental retardation from the neighboring churches. It was all right to have church groups visit these captive people in their hospital units, but they were not invited to attend worship on Sunday morning. Why were these people denied a chance to worship God with others? Second, I began to see the powerful combination of the creative arts and faith in the experiences of children with mental retardation. In singing with many of the children during the day, I was always amazed at the religious songs and ideas these children would express. I wondered how these ideas were implanted and nurtured in this otherwise secular environment. I soon discovered that in the evening, many of the children were rocked to sleep by women who would hum the familiar hymns of the church to them.

Fascinated by the religious educational questions coming out of the field experience, the journey continued in 1980 when I enrolled at Princeton Theological Seminary and studied with Dr. James Loder in hopes of finding some answers to the origin of faith among people with disabilities. I found out that not only did they not have the answers, but no one had asked the questions I was asking. I began to look at ways of better understanding this phenomenon as a chaplain's assistant, working with behaviorally disabled adolescents at Eastern State School and Hospital in Pennsylvania. These children and adolescents from the poorer urban and rural sections of Pennsylvania society, who had been physically or sexually abused and violated by family members and other members of their community, taught me more about the intricate complexity of the human condition than did many of my seminary classes.

In search of more understanding of the rich combination of religion, the creative arts, and people with disabilities, I went to Harvard Divinity School in Massachusetts in 1983. I was also ordained as a pastor in the Presbyterian Church (USA) while working in a small, inner-city congregation in East Boston, and as a therapist for adults with mental illness. In my work with the church I met the social problems of gentrification and immigration among the citizens I worked with in this community of immigrants. As a therapist, I was introduced to the plight of those with mental illnesses in an age when community mental health centers were their only salvation.

A memorable class at Harvard University was in community psychology with Dr. Richard Katz, where the focus was on the seemingly limitless power of religious communities in healing and transforming the lives of its members, as well as educating people in their respective faith, regardless of their abilities or limitations. In light of this class and my experiences as a pastor in East Boston, I began to wonder about the often untapped powers of care and love in congregations and parishes in welcoming all who wished to enter their doors.

Yearning for more understanding of this rich combination of faith, creative arts, people with disabilities, and communities of faith, I headed south on the journey to do my Ph.D. in special education at the University of North Carolina-Chapel Hill in 1985, with a focus in religious education at Duke Divinity School. My doctoral dissertation was an ethnographic study of people with developmental disabilities living in a religious community with nondisabled people. The context for this study was L'Arche Lambeth, a Christian community in London, England, where I observed and participated in the daily life of this gathering, seeing community, faith, and the creative arts blended together.

In this Christian community my vision of people with disabilities was radically altered as I no longer saw people with disabilities through the sole lens of the social scientific community. My vision was broadened, and in some ways restored as I came to see the lessons of life taught well by people whom society had labeled disabled. I learned the power of the sacred narrative when shared among others in thought, word, deed, dance, song, and laughter. I learned about the gift of patience, the virtue of caring friendship; the power of the Christian community to restore hope to those in deepest despair and depression; and the elastic yet fragile strength of God's love in holding this mortal body together. The teachers of these lessons were most often those whom society labeled "mentally retarded," not able-bodied assistants.

Finishing my doctoral dissertation in 1988, I went back to Whitworth College as an assistant professor in education in 1989. I soon found that there was no time at this small school, with a heavy teaching load, to conduct further studies in this area of work with disabled persons.

The journey of seeing did not end in Spokane. I was recruited to be the Director of Religious Life at Devereux Hospital and Children's Center, working with children with behavioral, emotional, and developmental disabilities. My approach in working with the children was educational: to create a community, a sacred space, in which the children could both learn and be nurtured by the religious narratives of their religious traditions and respective gatherings, and what it means in their own life.

Soon I discovered I was boxed in by the very title that I created. Many understood that I was to touch only the religious or spiritual issues in the life of these children and nothing else. Believing that one's mind, body, and spirit are basic characteristics of our fragile, mortal human condition, I have begun to truly understand and subsequently affirm the basic, spiritual experiences of life as supported by community, nurtured in relationships, guided by life's narratives, reinforced by rituals, enhanced by the creative arts, all in the company of saints of the church and God.

Listening and Watching

In compiling the essays and chapters of this book, I have tried to be faithful in arranging them as they have been written on certain resting places of the journey of seeing. There are two sections to this book. The first portion of this book is comprised of many of the first articles I wrote based upon conversations, experiences, and encounters with disabled persons (chapters 1 through 6). These encounters were unplanned and spontaneous meetings. It was the work and writings of the Harvard psychiatrist Robert Coles and the ideas about narratives and theological ethics of Stanley Hauerwas that caused me to reexamine my approach or stance in relationship to people with disabilities.

I started to listen and watch the people whom society had labeled disabled as living stories rather than as clients, patients, or students. The special educator Jim Paul challenged me to begin looking at those children and adolescents who were segregated into special education classes in public schools from the position of a theologian and religious educator rather than as another special educator.

In this spirit, I began to listen, watch, and be with others who were labeled by society as "disabled" from this different vantage point, standing and looking out from the church of Christ, trying to perceive and understand the differences among us from a theological perspective. It is with this perspective that I came to see creation anew in the life of Joshua[2] who plays the piano, Gene who draws revealing pictures of the Holy Spirit, Patty and her daughter Annie who taught me about the inseparable bond between family and church, members of the l'Arche Lambeth community who taught me about the necessity of celebrating life, and the parents of children with disabilities who have gathered at Montreat Retreat Center in North Carolina, teaching me about being the church of Christ when living with a disabled child.

The second section of this book (chapters 7 through 24) begins after I came into my role and function as the Director of the Religious Life program at Devereux Hospital and Children's Center of Florida. I was excited about blazing a new trail in the journey of *being with* disabled children. The educator and sociologist Parker Palmer helped me further by referring me to the biography of the Nobel scientist Barbara McClintock, *A Feeling for the Organism*. McClintock's extraordinary insights into biological genetics, as explored through corn, came through a simple approach: "One must have the time to look, the patience to 'hear what the material has to say to you,' the openness to 'let it come to you.' Above all, one must have 'a feeling for the organism.'"[3]

McClintock believed that no two corn plants are exactly alike. Because they are different, you have to know the difference. This involves not only an intellectual drive, but an emotional investment on the part of the researcher and writer.

McClintock's approach is what helped me the most in my work as the Director of Religious Life at Devereux Hospital and Children's Center of Florida. I was granted permission by the Devereux Institutional Center for Training and Research to conduct the Religious Narrative Research Project from 1991–1992, inquiring and collecting the narratives of the children and adolescents with disabilities, focusing primarily on the religious or spiritual experiences of the children. Having conducted an ethnographic study of a l'Arche community for my doctoral dissertation, I sought help in designing this study from the educational sociologist George Noblit and the religious educator John Westerhoff. I incorporated the ethnographic research methodology in collecting these stories, beginning with the traditional inquiry into their backgrounds and information regarding their "condition," or why they had been placed in this institution. I used interviewing techniques, asking all the young people questions about the nature of God, Satan, faith, and death, as well as asking them to draw pictures of God, heaven, and in more than one case, hell. (Like other young adolescents, Satanism, evil, and death were a big attraction among these children.)

However, the words of Barbara McClintock took life as I began my work at the hospital. In order to truly hear what these children had to say, I had to let them come to me, not me recruit them necessarily. This meant I had to be with them, day and night, whether in school or on the unit, in order to have a feeling for the spiritual journey that these children were on in life.

For the first four months of my journey at Devereux Hospital, I had the luxury of hanging out on the units, the school, and gym, the playground, the cafeteria, and the lake side. I did not tell anyone what I was doing on the unit floor unless they asked. I let them initiate the contact, rather than my doing the work. The word among the young people and staff that I was the pastor for the hospital, or as I was to be christened, "the Spiritual Religious Dude." They knew that I would visit the units once a day, six days a week, and that they could talk to me about a wide variety of subjects concerning God, life, and death without its being recorded in their medical records. Confidentiality was a must. By being there with the children and staff, trust was established, and relationships took off with this new community of friends. It was through being with these young people that they volunteered to be part of the Religious Narrative Study, wanting to share with others who read and hear their story that they know God, and have a desire to know God.

In getting a feel for these children, I came to appreciate that no two children and adolescents are exactly alike, no matter how similar their background, or psychological and medical assessment may be. I developed a passion for the different, the original, for those who are different in hopes of understanding them better, and the limitless variety of simply being human in the context of this community setting. While all these children had been labeled with the *same* or similar label of having a behavioral or emotional disability, and in some cases a developmental disability, it is safe to say that no two children or their respective journey was alike. I saw and came to know each of them as individual pilgrims who were lost and scared in the public square, in search of a community of care, be it the church or the synagogue.

Each one of these pilgrims had their own way of perceiving and relating to others in their community. For example, there is the young Jewish boy who wrote poetry to express his angst; the young boy who found God in listening to Motley Crue, a heavy-metal band; the sassy young woman who hit me in her angry turmoil; the pictorial world of a young boy from the south; the sharp, piercing fragments of a shattered life of another young boy; the decent, orderly world of one young woman; God's holy surprises in the life of Sal; the control of the Behavior Mod God in Steve's life; discovering Randy and *his* multicolored coat; George's encounter with the Lord, which is an adventure still unfolding; and the simple, resounding praise of God found in Jordie's life.

I have come to appreciate and know these individuals, with the knowledge of their labeled condition. As a music therapist and special educator, I have been well schooled in the science and art of labeling, categorizing, and educating children and adults with a wide variety of disabling conditions. What is different about the interpretation of these stories is that I have come to understand their stories no longer from the social scientific tradition alone, but against the background of the Christian community, and that has made all the difference. Rather than seeing a person as a label and category, with some point of reference to a family and a school, I look out of a community of faith to see where each person's place is within a synagogue or the church, or what the Apostle Paul described as the body of Christ. For these young children and adolescents are invaluable members in a community that longs to hear and appreciate their stories, meeting and welcoming them from their treacherous yet real journey of life. For they want to tell us their stories of God, as reflected in these narratives of faith, hope, and love that will bring us to a new understanding of our perception of and relationship to one another and God.

In the following narrative about Joshua, a piano player with a secret, I came to literally anticipate seeing the unique and different among children and adults whose labels barely scratched the surface of revealing the person hidden in the terminology. For in Joshua, I came to see that God plays piano, too.

1

God Plays Piano, Too

Besides everything else going on in creation, does God play piano, too? This question was met with a resounding yes! after I first heard Joshua play the piano. Joshua attends a public school in Spokane, Washington. He is a cute, healthy-looking six year-old boy who appears to be filled with high energy. But when you get physically, as well as emotionally, closer to him, you begin to see that there is something unique about Joshua. He is, by most assessments, autistic.

One way of describing autism is to say that it characterizes someone who is delayed in his or her mental and emotional development, displaying extremely structured and repetitive behavior. This disabling condition received great attention in the movie *Rain Man* with Dustin Hoffman's portrayal of Raymond, a middle-aged man with autism.

Like Raymond, Joshua repeats what you say three or four times. For example, I visited Joshua as part of my job as a special educator at Whitworth College. I greeted him for a music session by asking, "Does Joshua want to go play the piano with Brett today?" He replied, "Does Joshua want to go play piano with Brett today?" He then grabbed my hand and led me through the doors of the classroom down to the piano room.

We took a brisk walk down the hall and through the school gym, where a fourth-grade class was learning to throw a basketball. Children whispered "Hi," and secretly waved to Joshua as we ran over to a door on the opposite side of the gym. Plainly, Joshua was well known in this school. In a storeroom in back of the gym in this small cinder-block elementary school is an old Baldwin spinet piano. It is brought out for musical assemblies when the gym is used as an auditorium.

This dusty, cluttered storeroom is where the creative moment usually unveiled itself. Joshua, seeing the piano, got excited, asking, "Does Brett want to hear Joshua play the piano? Brett does?" I answered, "Play it." With that, Joshua jumped onto the bench, slid to the middle, threw back the wooden cover hiding the piano keys, and the transformation began.

Like an orchestra waiting for the conductor finally to come on stage, Joshua began randomly hitting a few notes. He was warming up in his own peculiar way, as if getting ready for God, the Conductor of Life, to come on stage to take a seat beside him. (Joshua only has peripheral vision and is unable to focus on what is directly in front of him. He turns his head in an awkward position so that his eyes can see the piano keys.) As he listened to the various notes his hands were playing, Joshua seemed to be searching for the correct keys for his first chord. The first chord would be the anchor for what was to come.

And suddenly, there it would be: Aha! Success! After the warm up Joshua mysteriously found the chords he had been looking for: C major, to G major, back to C major. Soon his feet were hitting the baseboard of the piano. With his feet he beat out the rhythm of the song he wanted to begin his recital with. Joshua kept a very steady beat, and, with his hands having found the right chords to play, began to sing his song, with perfect pitch and jazzy rhythm: "Baby, hold onto me . . . Baby, hold tight."

He played the song through once, then stopped, smiling, waiting for my applause. Then he asked me for the reward: "Brett writes it down? Write down the title of the song?" And with a red magic marker I wrote out the title in bold letters on a piece of paper. Joshua smiled and turned back to the piano to continue the recital: the theme song to the television show "M*A*S*H," "It's the Time of the Season for Loving," and three or four more songs I vaguely remembered hearing on the radio. I was amazed at Joshua's repertoire of songs.

There was one song we kept coming back to, a Phil Collins song, with lyrics that pose a serious question about this young boy's life. The song begins: "There must be some misunderstanding; there must be some kind of mistake." I began thinking that these words state the problem I have in understanding the puzzle of autism. God, who created us, probably agonizes over the plight of anyone who is autistic, a condition that cripples and limits a child's relationship with self and the world. But since there is autism in the lives of children, "there must be some misunderstanding; there must be some kind of mistake." Is Joshua's disabling condition a cosmic mistake? Or does Joshua's life present a new lesson about the inherent value of being created in the image of God?

After thirty minutes we came to the end of the session, which had ended not because Joshua was tired, but because he had to get back to class and I had to get back to the world of college students, which now seemed dull in comparison to such brilliance.

I have continued to ask the questions that haunt most of us when we are struck by the unusual, by what appears unfair: Why, God, does this happen? Why is Joshua, whose life has been riddled with such mental limitation, able to excel in this one domain, this one area of intelligence? How does he have this one splinter of talent? Here is Joshua, who is barely able to read a few sentences, who is not very communicative verbally, yet who is able, with great élan, to communicate musically with the world around him on an old elementary-school piano. Being with Joshua at the piano became my way of understanding how he experiences the world around him.

While Joshua appears to be unable to communicate consistently with others through verbal or written means, he has either chosen or has been given one, and only one from what we know, way to let his light shine: through music. Through the tool of the piano, which kindles his imagination, he tells his audience that he is aware of what is going on in the world around him.

Professionals working with mentally retarded or developmentally disabled children often ask what their worth is. Economically they never seem to be worth much; few will ever rise above a service job. It costs thousands of dollars to educate a child like Joshua. Chances are, Joshua will never graduate from high school, earn a "decent wage," or become much of a taxpayer.

However we should look beyond "accidents" and economics, and notice that there is something deeper going on in Joshua's life. His amazing talent should ignite those profound questions about life: Who has begun the process? Who has sparked this creative ability in Joshua's life? Who is the One who fills Joshua's life with music?

The One who seems to be conducting and playing through Joshua's life is the Creator. We read in Genesis of God's creating man and woman in God's own image—which means, in part, that we too have been made with the innate ability to create or to construct: to take the elements of God's creation, and bend and mold them until we fashion something unique in praise and service to God.

It is this aspect of creation that appears to be the driving, brilliant force in Joshua's young life. God's creative spirit is given a new twist, a new outlet, through the talent emerging in this young musician. God's creative spirit, alive within us all, has made it possible for Joshua to play the piano.

With this theological perspective we can begin to look anew at people with disabilities. What Joshua's life teaches us, amid our frantic search for justifying the cost of special education, is that the reason we nurture those who appear to be disabled is that they, too, are created in God's image. No disabled person's worth should be judged according to our frail, changing human standards. Instead, we all have dazzling worth in God's presence, in God's eyes, as we were created to worship and glorify the Creator. It is this ability that, remarkably, still seems intact in Joshua's life. Joshua's hidden talents reveal that he is able to praise God "with the stringed instrument [the piano] . . . let everything that breathes praise the Lord" (Psalm 150). Is not praise of God the reason why we were created?

Perhaps Joshua is not so disabled after all. Joshua sings and plays music in celebration of God's love for us all. Who knows? It may be God whom we hear playing the piano through Joshua.

2

Listen and Learn from Narratives That Tell a Story

While teaching a class on religious education with people who have disabling conditions, we read many narratives of people with various disabilities. There were books about people with mental illness[1] and narratives of people with physical disabilities.[2] But there were no narratives of people with mental retardation.

There are voices of families who have children with autism.[3] There are books by Jean Vanier and his stories of l'Arche, or the ark, a religious community for people with mental retardation.

The major problem is that first-person narratives of people with mental retardation have not been collected, heard, and understood by others. Without hearing their voice, we cannot understand their story. Instead, the nondisabled listener often tends to project what we think the person with mental retardation is thinking and feeling.

Second, when we project what we nondisabled listeners feel and think that a person with mental retardation would like, we assume the role of being their eyes, ears, and hands. They are no longer active participants in their lives; instead, they become objects of charity for whom we can do things.

Third, when we fail to hear the voice of people with mental retardation we tend to forget it exists, thus denying people with mental retardation the simple acknowledgment that they matter in our society. If we cannot hear the voice of those with mental retardation, then how can we include people with mental retardation in our congregations?

Hearing the voice of people with mental retardation is crucial for religious educators as we begin to develop curriculum for people with mental retardation. Much of our knowledge base for developing curriculum for young adults with mental retardation has come from curriculum for young children.[4] The problem with this approach is that while many young adults with mental retardation may have the mental age of young children, chronologically they are full of years of experience in life, which make them different than young children. Often, adults with mental retardation are treated like children, expected to color in coloring book pictures of Jesus while learning simple songs about the "B-I-B-L-E."[5]

One of the ways that we may possibly encounter people who are mentally retarded is to simply listen to their stories. This means consciously entering into a dialogue with another person, listening to the individual's story. Receiving that story is the essential first step in acknowledging the existence of another person, leading toward including the individual with mental retardation into our congregations as we all learn what it means to live as members of a faith community.

The importance of learning from first-person narratives how another person is perceiving life has been well documented by the psychiatrist Robert Coles. In his work with children we have begun to hear children's impressions about issues like morality and politics. He has revealed to us the concept of "child as citizen" who tries to live with the moral dilemmas of the world.[6]

The importance of first-person narratives, especially those of people with mental retardation, is the focus of this chapter. The narratives shared here come from people living in a l'Arche community in London, England. They reveal that those who are mentally retarded have their own ideas about life that are important for us to listen to in our learning to recognize their contribution in our congregations. The guides for this discussion come from two sources: the first is Robert Coles's work with children. These stories entertain us, cause us to reflect about what life was like as a child, and challenge us to learn new things from those who are kept quiet and often unseen.

The second guide will be narratives of people with mental retardation that I collected while conducting a study of l'Arche in London. By listening to the tales of people with mental retardation, we may begin to understand how better to welcome and include people with mental retardation in a congregation's life.

Robert Coles and the Story of Children

Robert Coles is a child psychiatrist, well known for his work with children. He is a storyteller who has collected the narratives of children around the world and put them in story form, from children living in the poor shacks of Brazil, to children living in the rural mountain communities of Appalachia in America. In his books on the moral and political lives of children, Coles records children's thoughts and feelings about the dilemmas facing them from fear of nuclear war to the power of racism in a black girl's life.[7]

Coles collected these narratives of children through "direct observation" rather than from a record of scientific experimentation, with comparisons and contrasts between children's responses in different countries.[8] He defends this method of interpreting a child's life rather than utilizing a sociometric test, because he does not want to be confused with those who give tests meant to measure certain kinds of abstract, moral thinking that will help researchers to "predict one's moral response to life events."[9] Coles sees himself as a clinician with patients who possess within themselves many truths. As a clinician, the heart of his work is listening and describing what has been heard, revealing stories children have to tell.[10]

Coles's hope is to uncover a "psychology of everyday life; a psychology of turmoil; a psychology of hope against hope with plenty of interludes of doubt and fear."[11] Coles believes these stories show that one cannot predict or know what will happen in life, or what our reaction will be to life's events.[12] Human life remains unpredictable. He makes observations about the mundane parts of life, plumbing the depths of the minor characters within the novels of human life. From this exploration he believes that familiarizing us with the larger, social dimensions that support the presence of moral and political thinking in children's lives will demonstrate the uniqueness of all life.[13]

Coles's belief about the unpredictable condition of human nature came by listening to children's narratives. He wrote that no one teaches children sociology, "yet children are constantly noticing who gets along with whom, and why."[14] Children are canny social observers and political analysts.

In the stories that Coles collects, three characteristics reveal, first, the entertainment or moral poignancy of stories that engage a reader. Second, endings to stories that leave questions, engaging the reader who may then reflect and enter a silent dialogue with the story. Third, the ethical complexities that face children in this modern world, where the adult is made the student, and the child is made the teacher.

The first characteristic is Coles's ability, as editor of the narratives, to pick stories that either entertain or reveal a morality that grips the reader's imagination. An entertaining tale of morality concerns Carlos, a poor child in the favelas or poverty slums in Brazil. Carlos's self-definition is linked to his view of wealthy people. He explains to his friend, Freddy, how the richer people have some of the same problems that the poor encounter in life:

> A rich kid once gave me a watch . . . he probably has five . . . I told Freddy . . . he's just trying to get through today and tomorrow, and he doesn't really have a grudge against people, against everyone.[15]

Once the reader is engaged in the story, Coles creates a silent dialogue with his audience. This dialogue is the second characteristic of Coles' stories. He uses these stories to describe abstract concepts like "character." He captures what character is about as described by a black woman teaching poor children in urban Atlanta, Georgia:

> But to me, character means an active person, who is ready to face the world, and make a mark on it. That's why I chose these kids. They're ready . . . to turn their backs on all their troubles and be good . . . be full of action.[16]

In this description about character, Coles forces the reader to reflect upon the stories that have been read in order to enter a silent dialogue with him about his understanding of these otherwise abstract concepts.

The third characteristic comes out of this dialogue and concerns a figure-ground reversal, where the adult, who is often the teacher to children, becomes the student, and the child becomes the teacher. This was the case with twelve year-old Sarann from Cambodia. She taught Coles, through a drawing of her home, about the importance of personal memory of war-torn Cambodia, giving her hope and security in a new land:

> A pond, trees near it, flowers aplenty, grass, a clear sky, a large and friendly sun . . . none of this imagery is very surprising or original—merely a child trying hard to retain a personal memory.[17]

These stories become a pathway into understanding the depth and unique character that each child exhibits when given the opportunity to express their thoughts and feelings. These stories in children's voices, edited by Coles, gain importance and meaning as they awaken the reader's consciousness in respecting the dignity of the children around us. Even though many children may say little, they appear to understand much of what is being said and done by those who consider themselves adults.[18]

Telling Stories and Empowering Voices

In looking at Coles's books, there were three characteristics of telling stories that captured the reader's attention and gave voice to children who are often seen but not heard. The first characteristic was the ability of stories to entertain us, raising tales of morality that cause the reader to reflect upon his or her understanding of life. The theologian Stanley Hauerwas writes that what makes a story good is its capacity to entertain: "We want to be drawn out of ourselves and literally rejoice in the lives of others which can be discovered through stories."[19]

But stories do more than entertain; stories help us gain some new understanding about life. They help to make sense out of what may seem chaotic experiences in life.[20] The stories that Coles tell portray children as modern-day heroes and heroines as they struggle against the odds to a glory that transcends threatening obstacles in which the reader can share. These stories may encourage the reader to associate with powerful forces that achieve success against a threatening world.[21]

Once engaged, the second characteristic concerns how these stories of children create a silent dialogue with the reader.[22] The writer Clara Park suggests that stories in books should create a silent dialogue between the reader and the author, where the reader should want to burst out his or her opinions about what is happening in the story.[23] Coles creates this silent dialogue with the reader by shaping the abstract concepts debated within many settings of higher education, not by a concise definition, but by children's narratives.

This is the case with his explanation of such terms as "character." Instead of giving a concise, abstract definition, Coles challenges the reader to relearn what the concept means by watching and listening to the stories of children who also live in a narrative world constructed by our stores.[24]

The third characteristic emerges out of this silent dialogue between the story and reader: there is often a figure-ground reversal, where the adult becomes a student in relationship with the child, who becomes the master of life. Coles writes that the psychiatrist Anna Freud encouraged her students to learn from children all they have to tell us, sorting out later how their ideas fit in with our own. Freud believed that these stories of children may help us with our own problems, those of theory, because there can be many clues for theory in what a child chooses to say to an adult listener.[25] By way of narrative, the children become the teachers instructing the adult learners, giving flesh to the adults' abstract concepts and theories.

These three general characteristics of stories, manifested in the work of Coles, give a powerfully meaningful voice to children. The stories reveal the thinking and feelings of children, providing the means of listening and entering a discourse with children, maybe leading to some insights into the problems we face as adults. Like children, people with mental retardation have also been placed in the category of being seen and not heard. Many times people with mental retardation are viewed as a mass of observable behaviors and sum of statistics in a textbook for special education, rather than as unique human beings created in the image of a loving God. People with mental retardation have much to share about their perception of life, which may give us some unique insights into our own problems and theories about life. The stories of people with mental retardation may also enable us to envision people with this condition anew as we begin hearing their life stories.

Narratives from l'Arche

The stories about life in l'Arche, told by people with mental retardation, come from a nine-month study of life in London's l'Arche community. In order to conduct a holistic study of a living community like l'Arche, describing a setting that is continually changing, the ethnographic method of research was chosen. The goal of ethnography is to describe the participants, rituals, interactions, and the physical setting so clearly the image produced is a verbal photograph.[26]

Ethnography is described as the research process in which, first, the researcher participates and observes life in the community. As participant, I experienced firsthand the daily rhythm of life in l'Arche from cooking meals to taking trips with other members of l'Arche around England. As observer, I listened to conversations and collected field notes and life histories of the past that people told me about l'Arche.[27]

The second essential part of ethnography is the collection of field notes. Field notes in ethnographic studies are essential in recording the daily life experiences of the people living in l'Arche. Field notes described where observations were taking place, the physical setting, and the social interaction, including direct quotes from people in l'Arche.[28]

The general goal of this study was to gain some insight into the characteristics of communal life like friendship, trust, care, the role of rituals, and the language of l'Arche. One of the surprises from this collection of material were the stories people with mental retardation told about the various aspects of life in l'Arche.

Listening to their stories I found some entertaining and engaging, told in a dialogical relationship where they were the master teller of life in l'Arche and I was their student observer, sharing new insights about life in l'Arche. It was revealing to hear how verbally articulate the people with mental retardation were about their thoughts and feelings. Most of the people living in the community were considered mildly to moderately mentally retarded. Their ability to articulate ideas about l'Arche become a key resource of this study about the nature of community. Once the friendships had been developed between the people with mental retardation and the researcher, I was allowed to listen to much of the gossip, tantrums, and jokes given by those with mental retardation to others in l'Arche.

The ability to verbally articulate thoughts and feelings by people with mental retardation revealed and reinforced the essential truth that these are human beings, created in the image of God, regardless of what society has labeled them. Many of these people were older than I am, and have lived lives of hope as well as great despair. Some lived in London during World War II, losing friends and family. Others have survived the rigors and abuse of impersonal treatment in institutions for people with mental retardation. Through these experiences they have much wisdom to share with the younger assistants living among them.

Not only did those with mental retardation have much wisdom, but they are also highly opinionated. They have opinions and want to make their own choice about what movie they want to see on television, and will tell you which pub they would have chosen to visit on Friday night while discussing their ideas about God and church. They have likes and dislikes, are friendly one moment and turned off at another moment. In other words, they are human beings, limited only by the opportunities those who are nondisabled give to them in l'Arche.

In this section are some of the thoughts and feelings people labeled "mentally handicapped" have about living in l'Arche Lambeth. Using the three characteristics present in Coles's stories of children, what follows are some of the narratives of people with mental retardation in l'Arche.

First, there is Beatrice's explanation of l'Arche, which, in reflection, I find engaging, entertaining, and insightful about community life. Beatrice talked about l'Arche as if it were a big vegetable patch. After drawing a picture of l'Arche, Beatrice told me exactly what she drew and what it meant for her:

> Apples, pears, potatoes, bananas, onions, and apples, potatoes, parsnips; community is like a vegetable patch. We cook all of these foods, nice foods, in community.

Later, when asking what Beatrice liked about living in l'Arche, this is what she shared: "They let you stay in bed when you're not well. They bring the food to you, they do. And they give you hot lemon tea." Beatrice also seems aware of her own shortcomings. One night she prayed to God: "Help me to be less stubborn, Lord."

Second, the stories people told me about their lives in l'Arche created a dialogue between us. One topic that fostered this dialogue had to do with the disavowal of their disabling condition. Many of the people with mental retardation said that they were not mentally "handicapped" or retarded. Beatrice was most emphatic about this point, telling me that she was not handicapped. Delia, who was mentally retarded and epileptic, was also sure that she was not handicapped. She said that the handicapped were hard to be with, "needing a lot of help, like getting to the lavatory [bathroom]."

But then there was Maggie, who had epilepsy and was mentally retarded, who said that she asked herself these questions about those who were nonhandicapped: "What were they going on about? What are they trying to say to me? It felt like another dog, an animal in the house." Dennis did not feel that some assistants liked him: "Sometimes

I don't like them. I feel that they're not like me. They're not nice to me, and I'm not nice to them."

This issue of one's acknowledgment of a disabling condition brings forth many questions and few answers, like why is it "good" or "right" for a person to know his or her disabling condition? If it is psychologically important for a person to know they have a disabling condition, when should we tell individuals of their condition? Who should tell them of their condition?

Third, there was a reversal of roles where those in the community understood that I, the researcher-assistant, was the student and they were the masters in l'Arche. There is Delia telling me that "community" is really "cumity": "It means the same thing that you mean but it's spelled differently. It's big, and has lots of people in it."

There was George who seemed to have an answer to all my inquiries. When asking about care, George patted me on my shoulder and said that "all of us care for each other, even you. We show care by helping with things, like shopping."

To Be Seen and Heard

Using the characteristics of stories found in Coles's work, the above narratives from people who, due to their disabling condition, have often been hidden from the larger society, are beginning to be heard. What I found was a group of people who have lived a good life in l'Arche. Their tales are engaging and entertaining clips from life in l'Arche, like the image of community as a vegetable patch. When being told the stories I was free to ask questions, and probed as deeply as I could into the life stories of these people who were clearly limited in some intellectual capacities. Many corrected me when I asked what it was like to live with people who were nonhandicapped. Because some who were mentally retarded saw themselves as nonhandicapped, I was given new insight into how people perceive themselves amid life at l'Arche.

Collecting narratives meant that I was to be the listener, for I was told how my idea of community is both the same and different from the concept of "cumity." What was interesting about the process of collecting theses narratives was that once friendship was established between myself and individuals with mental retardation, all I had to do was prepare a pot of tea and biscuits, nudge them a little bit about what I was looking for, and she or he would break out with a story about life. And, like all of us, as long as I gave them attention, the stories became more endearing yet complex.

Storytelling between a teller and a listener was a validation of the person who has a disabling condition. The act of telling the stories about life in l'Arche made those who told the stories hopeful, happy, secure, sometimes sad when remembering family members now departed, and many times angry and resentful of institutions. But it touched the storyteller and this author.

The reason these narratives have not been heard is because many of those with mental retardation have not been seen, except in walking on the street or in pictures from special education textbooks. When seen in these settings they remain apart from us. People with mental retardation have been almost absent from our social gatherings, and the public has been kept uninformed of their condition in society. This problem of not being able to communicate with those who are disabled has a social history as those who are not-yet-disabled people have kept people with mental retardation hidden in institutions in rural settings, or brought them into group homes but rarely visited them or invited them to our congregations, or left them to wander the streets of our cities as homeless citizens.

What this study reveals is that people with mental retardation are people. Like all other people, they have stories to tell about their lives. They await an opportunity to tell these tales to people who wish to listen. From these stories we may learn about how others see, feel, hear, and think about the world we are living in together.

Conclusion

Stories make meaning out of what may seem chaotic experiences in life. The voices of children and people with mental retardation are starting to be heard in our congregations through their stories. Experiences of including children in worship, reading Coles's books, and living in l'Arche with disabled persons confirm that these people within our society have something important to contribute to communities of faith.

In looking at the characteristics of stories used by Robert Coles, we are entertained and engaged, which in turn creates a silent dialogue between the author and reader, whereby the reader is taught about the worldview of a child. These three characteristics are not separate steps in a well-developed process of understanding the charm of a child's story. Instead, all these characteristics of stories work together in teaching us about the world through the lives of children.

Reflecting on the l'Arche narratives, friendship between the author and the storyteller had to be present for this research to work. If the people with mental retardation did not trust the researcher, then they would not say much about life. Most of the stories collected were told after the author was in l'Arche Lambeth for five months and friendships were established.

In reflecting upon the work of Robert Coles and the author's tales from l'Arche, there are two critical issues that need to be addressed. First, Coles and this researcher coauthor the texts of these stories on children's lives and tales of people with mental retardation, selecting stories that portray and defend their thinking about the world. This is an important screening, for no story is pure.[29] Stories are told to propose and defend a worldview. The anthropologist Edward Bruner writes that such studies, like these of the voices of children and people with disabling conditions, are coauthored because both the researchers and their subjects come to share the same narratives. Both Coles and this author come to live in the world of Carlos's Brazil or Beatrice's London, as these authors and their subjects come to share the same narratives. These authors and their subjects become "unwitting co-conspirators in a dialectical symbolic process."[30]

Second, what has not been covered in this article is the issue of alternative forms or methods of telling stories. While the written and verbal word can be used as a form of expression by most of us, children and those people with mental retardation are also capable of expressing their thoughts and feelings through other expressive mediums. In Coles's books there are numerous pictures drawn by children to communicate their story. In this author's work on l'Arche there are drawings by those with mental retardation, like Beatrice's drawing of the vegetable patch symbolic of community. While art speaks of everyday life, art also has a power all its own in the colors and shapes to create an atmosphere and communicate an idea.[31]

In closing, stories are educational. Like stories, religious education should also be entertaining and engaging, creating a dialogue with God in a community of faith, that moves and enlarges the participants' knowledge of God. God is alive in these stories, giving voice to those who have been shunted to the sidelines of life as "kids" or "retardates." They hold much wisdom and insight into life's troubles. We cannot live without them. God is active in all human life, regardless of one's years of experience in life or one's intelligence quotient.

The task of listening to and participating in the narratives of children and people with mental retardation is not only for trained psychiatrists and educational anthropologists. The discovery of these invaluable insights shared by those we least expect to receive it from comes by consciously being aware of life around us. Some ways that religious educators and pastors can begin discovering and collecting these insights is by spending time playing with, listening to, and watching the children and people with disabling conditions in our midst. It is by letting others be themselves, trusting enough in others to let them go and be free to interact and be with others, resisting the urge to isolate and dominate conversations and play, that the narratives and stories emerge. Often, listening and participating in the mundane activities of life, like shopping with a child in a store or going to the pub with a disabled person in London, is where many meaningful interactions occur. It is important to write down what is seen and heard, and record what we have also experienced as we capture revealing incidents that are soon memories.

With these conversations there will be some place to reflect and share with others our collection of wisdom-filled narratives. The result of this reflection in much of what Coles and this author experienced was a need to renegotiate expectations. For Coles, the children's narratives reminded him of the unpredictable nature of being human. For me, the narratives of people with mental retardation reminded me that their disabling condition is just that: a functional limitation that is part of their life as a human being. But this one limitation does not define or describe the whole person. Instead, listening to the stories of people with mental retardation reminded me of their humanity, helping me in relating to others, regardless of one's abilities or limitations, as children of God.

If we listen to these voices, then we may learn more about the life around us. We may become advocates, urging others to listen to each unique voice of a child or a person with a disabling condition. These are voices wanting to be heard. We should make way in our congregations for these voices, learning to live in community with these storytellers rather than waiting for them to make community with us.

3

Opening Windows

*In my Father's house are many rooms; if it were not so, would
I have told you that I go to prepare a place for you? And when
I go and prepare a place for you, I will come again and will
take you to myself, that where I am you may be also (John
14:2, RSV).*

I n recent years, the church has begun to confront the issue of how
best to welcome and include people with disabling conditions into
daily congregational life. Some churches have chosen to build wheel-
chair ramps into sanctuaries, while other churches have brought skilled
people into the congregations to use sign language for interpreting the
spoken sections of worship. But when focusing on the issue of including
a person who is severely or profoundly mentally retarded or a person
with schizophrenia, there has been little progress.

As an example, in one congregation where I was working as the
minister to the young people of the church, the church staff was grap-
pling with a request to provide services for a twelve year-old boy who
was severely mentally retarded and multiply disabled with cerebral palsy
and scoliosis, or curvature of the spine. When meeting with the mother
of the young boy, one member of the church staff stayed to talk about
setting up the nursery area for the boy while the family was in worship.
I, at the same time, talked about moving pews in the sanctuary so that
the boy could attend worship with the family. In the end, the boy was
placed downstairs in the nursery and never did attend worship.

When confronting the challenge of including a person with mental
retardation or a person with a mental illness, one of the persistent
questions is this: Will the person with a disabling condition understand

and appreciate worship? The underlying question is, "Will the person with a disabling condition do something embarrassing in worship, and what will they get out of worship if they cannot do anything during worship?" If the answer is that we do not know how much or what the person with a disabling condition understands in worship, and if we cannot control the reaction of the person in worship, and they cannot do anything in worship, like sing hymns or read creeds, then often the person with a disabling condition is taken to the nursery area of the church, or is not brought to church at all.

Another possible answer to these questions may be found in Gene's story. Gene, the son of a Methodist pastor, is a young man in his thirties who is mentally retarded and is also labeled schizophrenic. His mother was a housewife. He grew up as an only child in the rural countryside of western North Carolina. Gene lived at home for the first few years of life, attending the churches where his father served as pastor. Gene has been living in a state-run institution for the last twenty years due to his parents' inability to take care of him at home anymore, and the opportunities for further special schooling that were not available in his own hometown. Even though Gene has spent a great deal of his life in the institution, he spends most weekends with his family.

Gene is unique in that he possesses extraordinary graphic talents. His parents report that from an early age he drew unusual yet excellent pictures at home. In 1977 he became part of the fine arts program at a state institution in North Carolina. In recent years he has held several one-man shows, including one in which he was featured at the North Carolina Museum of Art. Critics have hailed his work for its sense of sophisticated simplicity, sensitive line, and unique usage of color.

In looking at the abilities of persons labeled "mentally retarded," Gene is one who fulfills yet challenges our understanding of that category and label. He fulfills that category because he appears to be slow in his ability to communicate verbally with others, and often seems childishly shy in being with other people. But Gene's hidden gifts now being discovered reveal a complex, talented artist.

Meeting with Gene once a week for six weeks, 30 to 45 minutes per session, I explored with Gene his perception of the Trinity: God, Jesus Christ, and the Holy Spirit as he drew their pictures on white paper with a pencil, and gave me a narrative about the persons in this triune communion. Sometimes Gene also drew a self-portrait, along with pictures of his mother or his late father, as well as of the interviewer.

Into our fourth week of interviews and drawing sessions, Gene baffled and surprised me with some new answers to the old questions I had been asking him. For four weeks, Gene had always drawn the Holy Spirit as a woman, usually with a dress on and long hair. I was ready to announce to the world within this institution that Gene perceives and imagines that the Holy Spirit is a woman.

But then Gene did something I was not prepared for: When I asked him to draw a picture of the Holy Spirit one day, he drew a picture of a house, with what looked like a storm over it. There were clouds over the small house, and lightening bolts coming out of the clouds with only the sound of thunder missing from the scene. After completing the drawing, I asked Gene about the image he had drawn: "Where's the Holy Spirit in this drawing?" Gene's response broke all the categorical stereotypes that I had fixed in my mind: "The Holy Spirit is the house who protects me against the storms in life. These are the clouds, and this is the rain, and this squiggle line, this is the lightening. I'm in the house with the Holy Spirit (protecting me)."

Clearly, Gene was not limited to one stereotyped impression of the characteristics of the Holy Spirit. Gene understood and was able to use a metaphor: "The Holy Spirit is a house who protects me against the storms in my life." I stopped the session there. Gene and I hugged each other, knowing there was little else that either of us could say or would dare to communicate for the rest of that day. We left to go on with our busy lives. For one brief moment, God's Spirit gave new light to the role and function of God's love as it became the house that protected both of us from the storms of daily life. A simple picture of a house with a storm outside communicated more than several hundred words about the nature and work of God's Spirit in our very human lives.

What happened? It was as if, to continue this metaphorical image of Gene's house, a window between his life and the world around him was suddenly wide open, the curtains thrown back, the screen raised, where Gene could look out into the world and I could look inside his life. This piece of artwork, this simple line drawing, became the vehicle by which we could communicate with one another, meeting each other at life's window. Gene gave me permission to look into his room of life, gaze upon some of the artifacts strewn around the room, and Gene held out to me a memento from his cluttered room, an image of God that challenged my preconceived, theologically informed image of God's Spirit. In the midst of the passage, his artistic offering transformed my understanding and image of God's Spirit.

This moment of sharing such intimate knowledge, a most precious moment, is rare between two people, especially with those whom society has labeled "mentally retarded." Part of our social understanding of this disabling condition is the observation that those who are mentally retarded are not as able as those who are nondisabled to use such metaphorical images, nor are "they" able to perceive, let alone use, such abstract thought processes due to their mental ability or mental age. But when one ventures from the realm of verbal and written concepts to the world of the creative arts, one's disability in using verbal and written concepts is not as relevant, meaningful, or as important as are one's abilities, gifts, or talents.

Another example where a window has been opened and a person has had the courage and the opportunity to look out into the world, letting other people from the world look in, comes from l'Arche Lambeth. This is the story of David. David is moderately mentally retarded, very shy, evading eye contact when one first meets him. When he first came to this community, he did as he was told: nothing less and nothing more. But soon after he came, he picked up a 500-piece puzzle. Within two days, he had completed the puzzle, to the amazement of the nondisabled community members. Watching him begin work on several puzzles revealed an underlying structure to this gift: David would put certain, similar pieces into little piles around the area where the puzzle came together. Going through all the bits and pieces, he soon established his little piles, and then methodically arranged the broken pieces into a whole. Soon, David was able to put together not only 500-piece puzzles, but 1000 to 1500 tiny, complex, intricate puzzle pieces.

One of the most touching moments for David and another community member came by accident. David had just completed a complex puzzle of one of the rose windows of Notre Dame Cathedral in Paris, France. A nondisabled community member carefully tried to pick up the completed puzzle in order to slide it into a frame for hanging on a wall for all to see. But it slipped from her hands, and all five hundred pieces of the puzzle cascaded to the ground. With guilty feelings, she went to David's room to explain what had just happened. His response surprised the other member who was expecting some angry reaction: instead he simply turned and hugged her! He helped her pick up the pieces of the puzzle, and within a few days, he had completed the puzzle again. And this time, it made it to the frame.

To those nondisabled members of l'Arche Lambeth, David also appeared to understand the meaning of some rituals in the community. During Good Friday, there is a gathering of the community in one of the l'Arche house living rooms. People come together around a six-foot wooden cross placed in the middle of the room, a purple sash wrapped around the cross, with nails protruding from the place where two hands and feet would have been nailed. Before anyone else moved, David slowly and quietly went to the cross and kissed the spot where the feet would have been nailed. Again, quietly, he returned to his place in the circle, with his head bowed for the next hour.

Gene's and David's presence would often be overlooked in the midst of the busy life of most congregations. Sometimes the person with mental retardation is silent in the crowd, sometimes too shy or merely unable to participate in the verbal cacophony surrounding the individual. This is why the person who is mentally retarded may be seen but not heard, because they just do not know how to enter our very verbal congregational life. Both Gene and David reveal that people with the disabling conditions of mental retardation have something to say to us: called into existence by the same love of God that brought us all into being, they exist in our midst as equals, as children of God. As children of God, people with the disabling condition of mental retardation not only exist, but their very existence is essential in the body of Christ. In the Gospel of John, Jesus uses the metaphor of the house, like Gene did, explaining to his followers that whoever is with God is in "his house." People with mental retardation are in God's house. What happened in the two stories shared in this chapter is that they opened up the closed windows in their rooms of life in God's house, and let us know they were already moved in, feeling quite at home.

It appears that some people with the disabling condition of mental retardation have not been asleep. They have been quietly observing us, watching and listening, surreptitiously participating in our discussions, and secretly have taken mental notes of the rituals and traditions within the church. Some have already discovered whose they are, realizing that the Holy Spirit, like a house, protects them from the storms of life. Others have seen and have known whose image is on the crosses in our churches, kissing the wood where the feet of Jesus would have been nailed.

Yet in congregations where the focus has been on coming to know God primarily by the literal understanding and verbal exegesis from the "Word of God," those people who are not able to communicate their thoughts and feelings successfully through those alternatives have often been shut out. Forgotten, they have been left to wander silently through the halls of churches.

The life stories we have read bring a new, exciting urgency to the task at hand: welcoming and including people with mental retardation into our congregations. The first task is to admit that there are many rooms "in my Father's house" that have yet to be identified or opened. Often our expectation is that people with mental retardation can *do* nothing, afraid that they will be bored, which causes us to forget that who we are as children of God is of much more importance to God. Other times we project our lives into their situations, worrying about what "they" will get out of worship, as if worship is judged a success by the economic, pragmatic model of "what I get out of it." We easily forget that our very creation by God was out of love: God created us to worship and glorify God by whatever means we can. If not verbally, then with the cymbals; if not poetically, then with the harp, timbrel, and lyre (see Psalm 150).

The second task is to nurture more open windows, where we can see and meet another person in a room once forgotten, where no one visits. The act of opening windows comes through caring, trusting, loving relationships with other people. As we come to know God through Christ, we also come to know the person with mental retardation. It may be through the act of drawing the Holy Spirit as a house, or by putting together a puzzle, framing it, and hanging it on the wall inside a house. Each person, being a unique creation of God's, has his or her own way of creating a connecting link, a thread of understanding and knowing, between the person in the room and another one standing on the other side of the window.

Opening the windows to once closed rooms in God's house is a perilous yet necessary venture, for our congregations are incomplete until *all* who wish to enter are welcomed as part of God's household of faith. Until we open the window, we stand outside, wondering who is on the other side, while the one inside feels shut off and shut out of life. Come, let us open the windows of God's house.

4

A Quilt of Compassion: The Disability-Affected Family and the Church

Participating in a childbirth class with five other couples who were expecting either their first or second baby, the one characteristic statement that was shared among all the couples was the hope that, no matter what sex their baby would be, he or she would be healthy and normal. This hope is a prayer among most couples and families.

However, this hope is not realized for many families. Some families are greeted with the crushing news after birth that "there is something wrong with the baby." Consider the following story of Jani and Scott (their real names). In 1972, she gave birth to her first child, Scott, who was brain damaged at birth (as a result of the cord around his neck; he suffered a lack of oxygen): "We were plunged into the medical arena and the dizzying merry-go-round of experts and specialists, tests, and surgeries, endless procedures, and forms to fill out." Since this was before the passage of P.L. 94–142, Education for All Handicapped Children Act, there was little offered in the surrounding school district, with even fewer early-intervention programs in place. The support of her Protestant congregation was minimal, with little to no outreach, she said, "I felt isolated, and God seemed very far away."

In 1974, her husband, unable to deal with a child who was disabled, began divorce proceedings. Her own family of origin began breaking apart with the divorce of her parents. The final calamity was the result of tests on Scott: "Our neurologist's prognosis was that Scott was hopelessly [mentally] retarded and it would be in our best interest to place him in an institution." At the end of the week, Jani's prayer was simply, "God, if you are there, show me." With that, she slept for the first time in four days.

The next day, she was invited to a Bible study where she met people who were able to come alongside "a very lonely, frightened, overwhelmed, but doggedly determined young woman: friends who could love Scott and me with God's unconditional love. By that eventful week, all of my illusions and props—church, husband, family, medical profession—vanished. I was in the crucible, unable to see my circumstances clearly or the steps to solutions, because of my own limited understanding."

Once Jani had found the support of this small group of Christians outside the church, the struggle she faced was working *within* the church community:

> I was recommitted not only to raising the awareness and love quotient to the need for ministry to families of [those with] developmental disabilities, but also to increasing the awareness of hidden woundedness and suffering of all kinds in others. I uncovered a prevailing surface attitude of denial: "We don't have any handicapped or developmentally disabled or suffering; there is no need." They [those disabled] were there, but invisible to the congregation, on inactive lists, or ignorant of the Gospel. For children like Scott, there was no appropriate curriculum for [those with mental retardation]. Scott and I made do with regular Sunday school classes, and I helped teach his class. Because this church was in transition with an interim pastor, no new programs could be initiated. This lasted for four years. Needs were put on hold.

Later on in Scott's life, in the midst of this group of Christians outside the church, Scott "received Christ. He made his commitment when he was thirteen years old—not a day behind what youth often do in the normal course in [many Protestant churches]." For Jani, God worked in her situation "in spite of the institutional church's inability to help my frustration. I have [since] forgiven the institutional church."

Jani's hope in sharing her story of her particular journey in life is that possibly, "in some miraculous way [we will] meet each others' deeply buried needs and will be a catalyst to crack the hard shell of our collective denial and ignorance of the powerfully living Christ."

Growing, Changing Needs of Families with Disabled Children

Jani's story is just an example that highlights the struggles and the successes that many families with disabled children have faced with their home congregation or parish, as well as other places within the social services safety net created for families with disabled children. Churches are comprised of the very same people who work with those with disabilities, whether they are special educators, nurses, social workers, psychologists, occupational and physical therapists, art and music therapists, or doctors. The problems many families with disabled children have encountered amid professional health service providers as well as the church are legion.

The writer Clara Park has written a moving account of raising her daughter, Elly, who is autistic, in the book *The Siege*, and the problems she has faced. She wrote that there has been an institutional, systemwide breakdown or failure: a failure of imagination: "For all their silent attention, the professionals were not able to realize our [the parents] thoughts and feelings."[1] The professionals were unable to understand that they were bound together with the parents on a common task: to better the life of the child with a disability. They failed to see that the parents were, and are, their indispensable partners in providing the best, overall treatment of the child.

One of the main themes that keeps arising in these works is the outright confrontational, almost antagonistic relationship that many families with disabled children experience with the professional health service provider field and the church. Consider what the social researchers Gliedman and Roth wrote in their book *The Unexpected Minority*:

> The parent's rights over the child take precedence over the professional's personal moral views. To put it bluntly, the professional exists to further the parent's vision of the handicapped [sic] child's future. Should the professional disagree, he has every right to try to *persuade* the parent to adopt a different view. He also has every right to give advice when the parent is confused and seeks guidance

and emotional support. But except in the most extreme instances of parental incompetence and brutality, such as child abuse, the professional has no right to use his immense moral and practical power to intimidate or to manipulate the parent.[2]

Among other professionals, there are also the mistaken assumptions that they make with regard to how the family experiences life with the child with a disabling condition like mental retardation. The special educator Parnel Wickham-Searl writes that some professionals think that such families are engaged in a neverending struggle to relieve devastating personal and social problems that accompany the presence of a child with a disability. These families are often viewed professionally by their weaknesses and deficits rather than by their resources and strength of character.[3] In other words, the professionals and lay people alike focus on only part of the family story or the family system, that which is the child labeled "disabled," and not the entire story or system that may be in greater need of care and treatment.

The theologian Stanley Hauerwas writes that even parents of children with disabilities are held in suspicion by *other* parents who think that the parents of a disabled child spend a lot of time with the disabled child just to assuage their guilt. This is even more the case for a woman who is thirty-five years-old or older who did not have amniocentesis and has a child with a disability. Such a mother may receive "outright hostility. After all, they should have known better and taken the appropriate steps."[4]

What has complicated the way that professionals work with families that have disabled children is the changing patterns of families, themselves. The traditional vision of the American family, with relatively clear boundaries, sharing a common residence and a shared name, has been undergoing extensive changes. Much has been made of the "new family" order in what some social critics are calling a "postmodern age." The term "postmodern" is being used to denote a new social consciousness that is emerging and touching the lives of families. Life for the postmodern family is unpredictable, often incongruous, and more stressful than ever before.[5] Families are being forced to see that there are many beliefs, multiple realities, and a plethora of worldviews to suit everyone's taste.[6] Into this world of multiple choices, the family itself is changing. A person may belong to what the psychologist Kenneth Gergen calls the "floating family, which comprises a relatively formless array of familial relationships in a continuous state of flux—like the foam that drifts upon the ocean waves dispersing and reforming as the currents move to and fro."[7] The affectionate ties of a person in a floating family are increased and scattered; one's significant others grow and extend beyond the physical and relational ties that once defined family. As many families have brought or abandoned their disabled children in institutions or group homes, the young people in these settings soon attach feelings normally saved for only other "family members" to care workers on the units or group homes.

These changes have caused confusion, regarding the social values, economic stability, and child-rearing responsibilities. The special educator Jim Paul writes that this is especially true for parents with children who are disabled.[8] It is such changing experiences with professionals, with other parents, with congregations and parishes, and society in general that has become the catalyst provoking a transformational change in the lives of many parents with disabled children. It has prompted many to take action, not only for themselves, but to see that other families with children with disabilities were going to be treated in a caring, just manner. The transition was from a private, family-centered world, to public life and advocacy on behalf of the child with a disability.[9]

What has happened in these families may be better understood by envisioning the family as a quilt, each piece unique in its own patterns of appliques, use of colors, size of the quilt itself, thickness of the batting, stitchery work, and the all-important border that holds or draws everything together in place. Into the preexisting quilt-in-progress comes a child with a disability. While in many families each child is unique, the needs of the child with a disability are so strangely different. The preplanned space for the child in the family quilt just does not fit where it was supposed to be. In many cases, there is a ragged hole that exists as the pain, suffering, and unbearable numbness that many families encounter in the birth of the disabled child threatens to undo the entire family quilt. The family tries to make the child fit without tearing the whole quilt apart, but there are too many days that are stressful upon everyone, including the child with a disability. There is now a sense of randomness and unpredictability that has come into the life of the family quilt, as each piece feels the urge to fly away, and many hands are needed to hold the existing squares together. The hands and threads that hold this quilt of many pieces of fabric need to be supported and strengthened so that the quilt does not come undone. The family quilt needs to be somehow bound together and anchored in place, no longer divided among itself.[10]

One place, amid one group of people where this thread may be tightened and strengthened and the quilt anchored is in the context of the larger community in which the family derives not only practical and social-emotional support, but spiritual support as well: the church. The congregation or parish itself is a collection of quilts of various shapes and sizes. What families with disabled children are asking for, in the midst of the many turbulent days in learning who is the child with a disabling condition, is something, somewhere that connects or anchors them with others.

The role and function of the church in the often chaotic, changing expectations of families and the surrounding cultural expectations is, to quote the social philosopher and critic Christopher Lasch, a "haven in a heartless world."[11] The value of such a community is practical, as well as emotional and spiritual. For it is in congregations and parishes, a people with a past history of persevering, who gather together out of their shared belief in a God who is immanently present but also transcends the chaos, that all people are able to gain insight into the dilemmas of life. In this context the conflicting and immediate pain and joy of life are expressed by the family. Yet they are also able to place these immediate experiences in the broader context that may give new meaning and a sense of order to what appears absurd and random. It is such a context like a congregation that reduced the stress and gave hope to Jani and what the writer Bern Ikeler calls an odd healthy family.

In the following sections, there will be a brief overview of the needs and concerns that families with disabled children may bring to their respective churches. This is followed by a discussion of the unique place that congregations and parishes have in the life of such families, and the role and function of the congregation in a family's life. For it is in the church that many families have found the hands that hold the pieces of their quilt together.

Pieces of the Quilt:
The Family and the Congregation

Bern Ikeler, a writer with cerebral palsy who is active in the Presbyterian Church (USA), writes that those who have a disability in the family have been known simply as "the handicapped." As such, they are seen as the devil's child. The stigma of having a visible disability has a way of penetrating all systems, including the family; "it is the sole banner flying above the family roof, stamped on their sweatshirts."[12]

Generally, what some families are searching for in their church is as follows:

1. "Being with" the Family

Congregations and parishes are comprised of people from all walks of life and all sorts of experiences. One thing that occurs in many churches when a disabled child is born is that many families have been surprised how many others there are within the congregation or parish who *also* have a child with a disability. With up to forty-five or fifty million people with a known disability in this country, it is safe to say there are others "out there" who may have an empathetic understanding and response to the new situation.

The church is present, first and foremost, to listen as a trusted friend. To be courageous enough to listen and experience the pain and the frustration of the entire family with a disabled child is an act of charity; an act of compassion. To *be with* and, in a metaphorical sense, *walk with* the family, rather than doing something *to* or *for* the family is most precious. There is little need for an extended conversation of all the details. Family members are consumed by all that many professionals require of them so that they need a place to just be themselves, with people who understand them and have no agenda for them. What many family members need is for others to listen, to offer a caring embrace, and to provide practical kinds of help.

Among the clergy and lay leaders of a congregation or parish there is the possibility of finding other groups of people scattered within the population of the community, to help the family think about their new situation rather than just feel it. There are many new and unknown issues that the family will have to quickly adjust to, and the congregation and parish may help the most by simply being there.

2. The Forum to Ask Hard Questions of God

One of the common experiences of many families with disabled children concerns questions pertaining to the very nature of God in relationship to the creation of a child with a disability. The questions about relationships fall under the whole issue of responsibility: Is anyone responsible for disabilities? If so, who is responsible for the creation of the child with a disability? Is it God's responsibility? The person with the disability? Or is it something brought upon the family because of what they did in their life, revealing the nature of God's divine wrath? Is it a case-by-case question? Is it an unanswerable question and therefore one we do not need to waste more time trying to answer? Many parents just feel that it is not fair that they have a child with a disability. Suddenly, instead of rejoicing at learning to read by age three or four, they will be thankful for the child who has bladder control by age twelve.[13]

All of these questions and issues of good and evil pivot around the presence of suffering and pain in the context of a God who is said to care and love us. The appropriate place where these critical questions should be raised, discussed, answered, and debated over is not in the public square, like the special education class or the therapist's office, but in the church. It alone should actually invite such painfully necessary questions of humanity and God.

People are bothered by the presence of one who is different from others, who has a disability, and there is the tendency among many to point to a disability as either the presence of evil or signs of a God who allows bad things to happen to good people.[14] The idea of pitting evil against a good God is known in theological circles as theodicy. It dwells on the point that if God is powerful and good, how can there be evil in the world? To quote the Old Testament theologian Walter Brueggemann, "either evil exists because God is not powerful enough to overrule it, or because God is not loving enough to use God's power in this way. To compromise in either direction is religiously inadequate and offers no satisfying response."[15]

3. Church as Sanctuary

Ikeler entitles one of the chapters in his book *Parenting Your Disabled Child* "Yes, We Are Odd."[16] In this chapter, he focuses on the tendency within society to stigmatize the one with a disability; to make the person with a disability an object of charity or pain; to lose sight of that which is human. In quoting the social critic Erving Goffman, Ikeler writes that society reacts to a disability as if it were a disgrace.[17]

What the family with a child with a disability is in need of is a sanctuary, a place of refuge and protection where they may be reminded that throughout life's journey with a disabled child, this child is a living, breathing, growing, human being who, by the way, has a disabling condition. They are not a disgrace. Many consider the one with a disability as "the handicapped" or "the mentally retarded," forgetting or simply not acknowledging that a human being is not a disabling condition. Instead, one *has* a disabling condition, along with other God-given abilities, gifts, and talents that are vital for the common good of the community he or she is part of and has meaning in.

This simple statement often gets lost within the ranks and counsel of many professional health service providers who place a medical record number on the child, focusing on the deficit, disorder, or the "deficiency." Some parents feel that they, themselves, are now part of the problem to be addressed. Unknowingly some professionals may thwart parents' attempts to find solutions to problems encountered with their children at home.[18] The tendency is to work with the child as a one- or two-dimensional object, a clinical case needing medical treatment, behavior modification, and therapy, rather than as a living subject we live and work with in our daily life.

For example, in the context of a congregation or parish, as recorded in both Hebrew scriptures and the New Testament, all persons, regardless of what they can and cannot do, are reminded that their worth is not based upon their actions, but is found in being created by God. The naturalist Annie Dillard writes that the importance of human beings to God is that they are the ones who are living, who alone can praise God.[19] No one who is human is perfect, and all goodness in the presence of God, as witnessed by one's respective religious community, is limited, for only God is good.

The Role and Function of the Clergy

The family therapist and rabbi Edwin Friedman, in his book *Generation to Generation*, looks both at family systems as well as systems within congregational life.[20] Friedman believes that an important aspect of working with families is how we interpret and understand what is happening in the world around us, or our own self in this world; in other words, to see how everyone functions together within the family or the congregation. In empowering families to work with and overcome the sense of crisis like the unexpected birth of a disabled child, the family is in need of a vision of hope that they will be able to transcend the anxiety of the moment.[21] Without this vision of hope, then the family may be more deeply enmeshed and controlled by the crisis rather than having some control and sense of order in the seemingly random experience of having a disabled child.

In this regard, the clergyperson, representing a congregation or parish, has a unique vantage point in understanding families with disabled children in the following ways:

1. The Unique Entree of the Clergyperson

Friedman writes that "no other member of society is in a better position to foster these existential encouragements to healing than the clergy because of the unique entree into family systems our community position has given clergy."[22] Who else is with a family for some of the most important ritualistic occasions in family life like a minister, rabbi, priest, or nun? The designated leaders in religious communities are actively present and usually presiding over such rituals as baptisms, confirmations, bar and bat mitzvahs, weddings, and funerals that pertain to the specific family, as well as celebrating communitywide holidays such as Passover (Jewish), Christmas and Easter (Christian).

2. Knowledge of the Whole Family System

While the clergyperson is active in the many rituals with the family, he or she also has entree not only with one generation of the family, "but with the multigenerational processes of families that are just not available to any other member of the helping profession no matter what their training or skill. This entree gives the clergyperson unusual therapeutic potential."[23]

What is important about this multigenerational aspect is the belief among many family therapists that how the immediate family responds to a crisis in the family is a response learned from the preceding generation of the family, along with the addition of extended family members. The family therapist Carl Whitaker, when working with families, tries to include in the therapeutic session not only the immediate family, but as many members of the extended family as possible, representing the multigenerational nature of all families in order to better understand how and why the family responds the way that it does to a crisis such as a disabled child's birth.[24]

3. Length of Time Knowing the Family

Many clergypeople have an intimate knowledge of families, which sometimes spans more than one generation, and all the noncounseling experiences that clergy share with the family.[25] Not only has the clergy-person seen the family before in a crisis situation, but they will have also been with the family during the times when it is not as over-wrought with pain and suffering.

In conclusion, the clergyperson, unlike anyone else among profes-sional health service providers, is in a unique position to appreciate and promote the healing power of natural family resources and the church, helping the family realize that the birth and presence of a disabled child cannot alone undo a family. What gives the clergyperson the authority and responsibility to act in this way is that, in most congregations and parishes, the rabbi, minister, or priest is their leader. What they say and do can, itself, be a therapeutic modality.

The Dialogue Between a Family and Congregation

Having outlined the needs and concerns of the family that may be best addressed by their respective religious communities, and the unique role of clergypeople in the life of the family, the other important issue to be addressed is the powerful educational dialogue that goes on between the family and the congregation or parish they are part of. It is an essential opportunity and experience for the church to welcome and accept the family, for it provides the catalytic learning experience in teaching the religious community to be a caring, diverse, gathering; a quilt like no other in this world.

1. To Teach the Congregation about Care

It is fairly safe to say that no one is born a parent, but that one learns to be a parent(s) from one's children. Being a parent is not a natural role. While children learn much about life by listening and hearing adults talk and seeing how they relate to each other and other people in the world, the child also teaches his or her mother and father about the responsibilities of parenthood.[26] This responsibility increases and becomes even more intense with a disabled child.[27]

What disabled children teach their parents and siblings is the art of care and compassion; the ability to put aside one's own wants and desires in service to another person out of a sense of responsibility. What is essentially different about the family with a disabled child is that the child is often feared as one who is different; one who is not a gift but a threat to the "normal" way of life. These parents stand as a beacon, reminding other parents what it is to be a caring, loving parent, no matter what their child is like.[28]

In the same manner, churches need these families. No congregation or parish naturally has either the skills or resources necessary in welcoming and accepting children or adults with disabilities and their families. It too must learn to be a caring, compassionate, empathetic, and inclusive community of Christians or Jews. Those who may best teach the congregation to be caring are often these families.

The life lessons in learning to truly care for such families are not as easy as putting in a can of soup for the congregation's soup kitchen once a month. Society's influence on what is right and normal will increasingly encroach itself upon a congregation. Many will ask others in the community if it is worth the money and resources in rebuilding parts of a sanctuary for welcoming those with disabilities. The family with a disabled child will need to be consistently present and in the midst of the congregation and parish, and in being there will teach the other members that this is a place where compassion *should* begin, *should* be taught, and *should* be practiced.

2. To Teach the Congregation About Diversity

In learning to be a congregation of care and compassion, Hauerwas writes that our commitment to having those with mental retardation in our society embodies a richer sense of community than the language of equality provides. People with mental retardation call us towards being a community of diversity, where our differences help each of us to flourish exactly as different people.[29] What is important in celebrating this differentness is that the congregation and parish does so without excuses or regrets, but with an air of celebration.

Diversity is necessary for congregations and parishes to flourish, for they remind many in churches of the belief that God accepts them not for what they do in this world, but for who they are as creatures created by God. Christians believe that God affirms everything that is genuinely human.[30] Maintaining this diversity within the community is not easy; it is hard to sustain because people naturally fear differences. If those who are different will not change, then it may be necessary that they not live at all. Writes Hauerwas: "thus, whites fear blacks, men fear women, and all of us fear [those who are mentally] retarded."[31]

Blest be the Tie That Binds

Many families with disabled children have a need to be a part of, to place their quilt of a family, into the larger, comforting, caring quilts of congregations and parishes. Churches, in kind, need to include these families, for they bring into these holy gatherings participants who represent the natural diversity of what Christians believe is God's creation. Their quilt adds to the beauty and intricacy of the larger fabric, and does not distract anyone's attention or appreciation for the masterpiece in progress.

One of the missions that the church is uniquely qualified to address, unlike any other support group or social service connection, is to be in solidarity in mind, body, and spirit with their brothers and sisters who are disabled and their family and friends.[32] In being in solidarity with others, being with others who are considered disabled in the world, there is the binding thread that holds the family quilt together, as well as enhancing the very life of the church itself. To quote the Christian hymn: "Blest be the tie that binds our hearts in Christian love: the fellowship of kindred minds is like to that above" (John Fawcett).

The "tie that binds" families together, regardless of the family makeup, is the fellowship that is gathered together of people eager to connect and attach themselves to likeminded others in faith and experiences of this world and God. The social critic Christopher Lasch wrote that all families need to attach themselves to specific places and people, not to "abstract ideals of universal human rights. We love particular men and women, not humanity in general."[33] This is what Jani was looking for as she was singly responsible for Scott's care and well-being: a place of welcome that would accept her and her son Scott.

What the congregational and parish quilt does is join together the many lives of different and extraordinary people into a quilt of compassion. Throughout time, members of churches have come together not because of their differences but because of their common need and task. To be part of a community of people who care for one another not because it is the right thing to do, but because that is the way they believe that their God who loves them would want it to be. In response to the idea of God's encompassing love, by coming together out of this common belief, they discover the beauty inherent in the diversity and love of the people gathered together.

5

The Prophetic Voice of Parents with Disabled Children

I will pour out my Spirit upon all flesh; your sons and your daughters shall prophesy (Joel 2:28).

Who is a prophet? The Presbyterian minister and writer Frederick Buechner wrote that no prophet ever asked for the job, but was chosen by God. God puts a finger on someone, and the rest is history.[1] The Old Testament scholar Bernhard Anderson wrote that many prophets stood up for God against rulers, telling people about God's deep concern regarding humankind's sinful actions.[2] In taking their stand, God's prophets were perceived by others as people gone mad. Jesus regretted that prophets had no honor in their hometown, even among kin in their own home (Mark 6:4).

In listening to parents who have children with disabilities, I believe I have heard the prophetic voice emerge as these people tell their stories of churches that would not accept them or their disabled children. Like the Hebrew prophets, these families did not "choose" to have a disabled child. They thought that having a disabled child is more likely to make one feel crazy. Yet once their lives were changed by a disabled child's presence, these families have endured mixed blessings in their relationship with church leaders and friends.

In a more important way, like the prophets, parents with children who are disabled often stand up in our congregations and parishes, calling us to consider what it truly means to be parents and families as God's people. Some church members tell the family to be quiet and sit down, warning them of being too single-minded and obsessed about their disabled child. But these parents, embracing a child who is often far from what the rest of society would call "normal," have caused the rest of us to reflect upon our commitment to our children. Parents of disabled children demonstrate to others how much *every* child is totally dependent upon the health and security of the home. What helps center and anchor the family in the midst of the swirling, chaotic times of caring for and living with the unpredictable disabled child is God's gathering. God strives to embrace the family with disabled children through the members of Christ's body who are gathered together. But as broken people, all of us seek healing in God through prayer and worship. The struggle is often getting the church to respond in a caring manner to the family's pragmatic and spiritual needs.

I heard the prophetic voice of a parent with a disabled child after a workshop I gave on the church and persons with disabilities. I recently met Patty. She has, in her neck of the woods in the Pacific northwest, "moved mountains." Patty's faith in Jesus' love for her daughter (twelve year-old Annie who is autistic) has finally succeeded in getting the state and her local church to work with her and her family in making this a more hospitable world for Annie.

Patty is in her thirties and is a mother of six children. She lives with her husband and the children in a small house, set on a dirt road, near the Washington-Idaho border. The house is often hot inside during the winter, a wood-burning stove pumping out heat. Overall, the house looks a bit battle worn. It could use a coat of paint or two outside. Inside, the tan-colored carpet is water damaged and, in some spots, makes a squishing noise. It is wet all too often from an autistic child's fascination and play with shampoo and water. The walls look battle scarred where Annie has kicked holes in them. There are also places where Annie has stripped bits of the sheet rock off the wall and, along with many household items, has thrown them around the house. Patty said that so much is flying around the house some days that it seems as if the house, itself, is turning in mid-air. Many bathroom and bedroom doors are now locked with elaborate electronic computer locks, and even the refrigerator and kitchen cabinets are kept locked.

As I went into the house to talk with Patty and meet Annie, Annie was taking the hand of her younger brother, leading him off into the kitchen so that he could get her some food from the locked cabinets. She grunts and quickly passes by me while the rest of the family stops to greet the stranger. Soon, Don, part of the transportation team for Annie and a member of Patty's church, comes to take Annie to the nearby institution for what Patty's family calls a "weekend of normality." Annie goes away to "respite care," and the other children can invite their friends over without having to explain their autistic sister.

This past weekend, with Annie home for Easter, was exciting to say the least. It was a warm Holy Saturday afternoon when Annie suddenly was nowhere to be found: she had simply vanished somewhere into the heavy forest bordering their backyard. Annie's parents quickly called the nearest, and the most logical, helpers: the members of their church's prayer chain. All fifty members showed up within an hour and began searching for Annie. Patty, frightened for Annie's safety, heard coyotes cry in the surrounding wilderness.

Patty's mother in Spokane asked her church's prayer chain to pray for hope in finding the child. Patty's mother-in-law's job was to call the nearest neighbor. By mistake, in calling someone else to help search, Patty called the sheriff at his home. He too came out to help find Annie.

What made this search far harder than other searches was Annie's autistic behavior. Unlike children who can and will respond to the calling of their name, Annie simply does not respond to human commands. She would rather be engaged in a self-stimulating activity than obey someone's commands.

During the search, Patty was busy taking care of feeding the fifty people who were there to help find Annie. One friend asked if she had been praying, but Patty said that she had been too busy feeding the people who suddenly descended upon her house. When she did get a chance to pray, she told God that, even though there were times that she would be more than glad to let go of Annie, this was not the best of all times! Her prayer was, "Please God, I'm not ready to give her up yet. Washington has just started providing services for Annie; you can't take her yet!" Patty then remembered God's sacrifice of Jesus on Good Friday. "But that's what I did; I lost my Son for you." Strangely, Patty felt at peace: God, too knew what it was like to lose one's precious child.

Immediately after praying, before anyone could call the area's search and rescue team, the adhoc prayer chain search team found Annie. She was innocently playing in the forest. Patty's child had not been taken from her yet. Annie was fine. After celebrating the discovery of the lost child with her friends, Patty claimed that it was her faith in God, and the dependability and commitment of her church family, that had most helped her and her family move through these anxious, draining times of despair to a celebration of unbounded joy.

When I asked Patty about some of the lessons she had learned in living with Annie throughout the years, discovering who Annie is as a child with autism, Patty was ready with answers. She began with a quote by Paul from First Corinthians, where he was talking about the refining fire that reveals precious gold (1 Cor. 3:13). Patty senses that God is moving in her family as life with Annie is like a refining fire, revealing the golden quality of the family's character and faith in God.

A further lesson comes with another question she has heard: "What do you expect in heaven?" "I just tell them, 'Rest!' That's all. Rest!" Patty has been a hard-working advocate for Annie, whether it is securing funds from the state in buying the necessary equipment for Annie's education, or asking the prayer chain to help search for Annie. Patty simply wants to make sure that Annie can be who God created her to be. "Is that too much to ask of the state and the church?" Patty asks.

Another lesson in Patty's life is learning to see Annie as a blessing. Patty told me that the blessing is truly going to come from God in the end because Annie is so unlike other children, even children with Down's syndrome: "At least kids with Down's can *show* you love. Annie can't even show love like a normal kid or a kid with Down's! But I know that God will pay me back for taking good care of Annie."

The final lesson for Patty has been finding and using her prophetic voice for other families with children who are disabled in calling the state to meet the needs of her family and daughter. More than once she has had to call on the state just to meet the basic needs of her daughter, whether it is in-home care or specially adaptive equipment:

> God is using me and Annie. She's the way she is so that I can blaze a new trail or path for her and others. God is using me, and us, for opening up a lot of doors for others.
>
> For example, there's PAVE, Parent Advocates for Vocational Education. The director, when I ask for help, says that they listen to me because I'm ten steps ahead of them. You've got to think as a Christian. I want to know what to do. If God wants it done, then God will get it done. I couldn't get to where I am today without God.

After telling me all that she and the family have learned, Patty sat back, reflected, and said so much has happened since Annie came into their lives:

> But it's how we live. Annie is just part of our life. We've gone past the "Oh, my God" part of grief, and now we are onto the business at hand. It happened, and I can't make it go away. But I can be responsible from this moment on. If she dies, then I'll at least know I did the best I could do; I couldn't do any more.

What has kept the family together in learning to live the unpredictable life with Annie? The church. Yet not all churches have been welcoming. Patty has heard more than once, as have other families with disabled children, the pastor, priest, or some lay leader "politely" say to them, "I don't think this is the right church for you to worship in!"

In this rural part of Washington, Patty's family has found a church home, a small Mennonite congregation, that has willingly been crafted by God and Patty's family into a loving, caring community that truly accepts Annie as a child of God. With Patty's commitment to raising her *whole* family in the life of a church, Patty, Annie, and the congregation have learned to accept and be with one another in love. Now and then, Annie is quite "charismatic" as she has gone running in front of the sanctuary, gaily dancing around the pulpit with the preacher still preaching. Usually, she is solemn and quiet during silent prayers, but sometimes she quite freely verbalizes her prayers with a string of incoherent garbled vowels and consonants. Annie has also been known for simply deserting her family in church, going downstairs to the nursery and quickly stripping off all her clothes. Patty told me that once when this happened, a family who attended the church just glanced into the nursery, saw Annie, and then kept marching to the sanctuary while shielding their eyes saying, "Yep, Annie's in church." Even at the potlucks, the members let Annie go first in line for the food. They also accept the marvelous, unique creations she makes during the vacation Bible school as she ignores the rest of the children and the more mundane curricular activities.

To get the congregation to welcome Annie, Patty's prophetic voice has been heard by others as an irritating, squeaking wheel. Attending many conferences with heads of institutions for people with disabilities,

Patty discovered that the way these leaders got attention was exactly by being a squeaky wheel. In the church, Patty has "squeaked," calling the members to accept Annie and the family as they are. Why? Because Patty's family truly needs the practical support of searching for a missing child, the caring embrace of God's Spirit after a long week of fighting battles with the state, and the loving reassurance of Christ's people that the family is in the palm of God's hand.

What has the church learned? It has learned about the brief, bright glimpses of joy among the generally frustrating, dark moments of being a family with a child who is disabled. In truth, the church has learned what it means to be committed to parents with children who are disabled, no matter what the family may look, sound, and act like. And if the disabled child is to be nurtured in the home with the love of the family, then the family's faith needs to be nurtured by the gracious, loving support of God through God's people so that they will not fall apart. For if the family goes under from the challenge of raising a child with a disability, then so will the child.

Patty's prophetic voice has been heard by many. She has stood up for Annie out of the knowledge that Annie is one of God's children in need of a church home. Representing her family, including a child with a disability, Patty has taken the lonely stand against the state and church when it is done in the name of securing a hopeful future for Annie. Patty, Annie, and the family have blazed new trails in the state system in helping other families. Even more importantly, Patty's and Annie's prophetic journey has enabled God's people to learn how to invite, welcome, and accept the family and the child whose story is uniquely unfolding in the midst of God's story of love.

Like the Hebrew prophets, Patty did not choose this life. She is not busy questioning God about why a child with autism was born in her family. There are no easy answers to raising a child with autism. Yet deep in her heart, Patty knows that God loves her and loves Annie. Patty gladly accepts the responsibility of Annie's care from here on out. And what does Patty want God to know about her work with Annie? "I did the best I could do; I couldn't do any more."

6

Welcoming Unexpected Guests to the Banquet

It is a cool summer morning in the hills surrounding Montreat, North Carolina, as parents gather together to share something they have in common: a child with a disabling condition. The topic of discussion for this gathering has to do with how their individual congregations first responded to the presence of their child with a disability. The parents' responses echoed one another as they told of congregations who, though scared at first, learned to at least accept that the couple had a child with a disabling condition. Most of the parents learned how to work with their churches so that their child had a place in Sunday school, youth groups, and worship. Karen, whose two children have cerebral palsy and developmental problems, shared that her congregation has grown to accept her children and involve them in the life of the church. But Joy, whose son has Down's syndrome, said that the support was fragile at best. She handles the fragile support by no longer expecting much from the church but expecting much from God to care for her and her family.

Other parents of children with disabilities and adults with disabilities have experienced the church's fragile support. Many people with disabling conditions are angry at their church for what feels like a lack of caring support, a feeling that carries over to their relationship with God. Some people with disabilities feel that "if a healthy child is a perfect miracle of God, who created the imperfect child?"[1] For the writer Bern Ikeler, the whole family questioned and cried to the Creator: "What is happening to us?" Born with cerebral palsy, Bern's birth was the death of the family's dream child. Unlike a child's physical death, a disability is a death that happens hundreds of times each day, as the child is unable to do what "normal" children could do.[2]

It is not only those intimately connected with a person's disabling conditions who have felt the fragility of support. Church leaders have also admitted that their support is fragile. Many say they do not know what to say or do for the family of the disabled person. Continually afraid of saying something offensive at the wrong time, offering help not needed, some choose to say and do nothing at all. Practical signs of support are absent, the comforting words of care needing to be expressed are rarely heard, and the gift of being present in the challenging times in a disabled person's life is withheld.

This reaction is not isolated to churches. We live in a society that has created a mistaken belief that shapes our collective perception, or misperception, of disabled people. We have been lured to believe that having a disabling condition means one is less than fully human, regardless of what combination of gifts and talents a person might have. People focus on one's physical, mental, or sensory limitations. The person with a disabling condition is a provocative, painful sign of our own mortal condition and something that we would rather deny than accept.[3] As the theologian Stanley Hauerwas writes, the natural response to the misperceived stereotype that disabled people are in pain is to get away from the person as quickly as possible.[4] Such pain, or illusion of pain, is a threat to our communities.

Misperception of people with disabling conditions in congregations is not an individual problem, but is a dark, knotted, disturbing thread that runs throughout the richly textured fabric of congregational life. The challenge for the church is to rightly perceive that some people have physical, mental, or sensory conditions that naturally impose real limitations in terms of what some can and cannot do in life. Members of Christ's community are to look *through* and *beyond* one's abilities or disabilities into the heart of the other person as we come to be with that person, whether in times of exuberant celebration or righteous anger. We are called to live with one another as a sign of God's grace.

The gospel message affirms this message of grace in Jesus' call to love God with our whole being, and to love one's neighbor as oneself (Matt. 22:39). Overt exclusion of another person in God's family, regardless of one's abilities or limitations, hurts and offends everyone in the body of Christ. Jesus emphasized that Christians share a spiritual bond of loving care with one another that transcends our own precious, natural kinship network. Jesus points to the existence of a spiritually ordered community of neighbors, where we view ourselves as selves-embedded-in-community, rather than disconnected individuals living in the selfish and unjust order of the scarcity paradigm.

The Scarcity Paradigm

The anthropologist Richard Katz wrote that the scarcity paradigm assumes we live in a world of scarce, nonrenewable resources, and only those who are rich or powerful enough may accumulate and control the distribution of these resources. Such resources include items like oil, water, and health care provisions for people with disabilities.[5] Some even perceive of love as a scarce resource, fearful that they may squander it in the wrong places, thus using it all with no love left in reserve for an emergency. They are not aware that this is backward thinking, for in reality, the more we share love with one another, the more we have of it.[6] The scarcity paradigm is a justified description of our contemporary American culture. From such cultural pressures, none of us are exempt, including those of us who consider themselves members of Christ's body.

Juxtaposed with the scarcity paradigm of society is the alternative spiritually ordered community of caring love found in Jesus' vivid description of God's kingdom. Throughout the Gospel accounts, Jesus keeps pointing his disciples to the powerful reality of God's kingdom, the embodiment of a paradigm of abundance. The theologian Lesslie Newbigin suggests that the church on earth, called into existence by God in Christ, is a signpost on the arduous journey of faith, pointing out the eventual, glorious destination to the faithful followers of Jesus.[7] Yet Jesus' vision of God's kingdom provides a different lens on reality, a new spiritually ordered lifestyle that we should be committed to living out in this time and place. The church is called by God in Christ to live life on earth with an eye on this kingdom whenever we pray the Lord's prayer: "Thy kingdom come, thy will be done, on earth as it is in heaven" (Matt. 6:10, RSV).

In telling his followers about God's kingdom, Jesus used many parables, metaphors, and analogies. One parable that reveals the inclusive nature of God's kingdom is that of the great banquet feast (Luke 14:15–24, NIV). In this parable, Jesus takes the Old Testament image of the Messianic banquet, which is prepared and hosted by Yahweh, surrounded by the leaders and prophets of the children of Israel, and uses this banquet as the symbolic metaphor for God's kingdom, with God as the host and Jesus as the servant.

To summarize the story, the host has invited three prominent, wealthy men, and probably their families, to come to a large banquet he has prepared. But they all refuse him: they are all too busy with their ordinary lives to take time to accept the gracious invitation of the host to this most delicious love feast. The claim of God, the host, upon their lives was crowded out by the things of this world. The host, angry at such a response, tells the servant, "Go out at once into the streets and lanes of the town and bring in the poor and maimed and blind and lame" (v. 21). This most likely included the outcasts of Jewish society, like those people from the leper colonies, those who sat at the city gates and begged for money, and those who stole from others along the dark alley ways of Jerusalem to support themselves. At first, many probably stalled because they did not feel worthy and, in feeling unworthy, declined the invitation. The host then tells the servant to *compel* the people to come "that my house may be filled" (v. 23).

In verse 24, the host tells the servant the theological point of the story: None of those who were first invited will taste my dinner. But it is not by God's choice to exclude them, for the invited guests excluded themselves from the banquet. Vacancies have been filled by those seen as the most unlikely, unworthy, unexpecting guests at this feast: the poor, disabled outcasts of Jewish society. By turning to these rejected, disabled citizens, those who hid along the highways and the hedges, God transforms them from unwanted social outcasts to wanted, honored, though unexpected guests in God's kingdom.

Are those who are disabled in this story symbolic just of those who are obviously disabled in our time and place? I think not. Those who are disabled in this story represent all humankind. The people who are disabled represent all who come before God every Sunday, all too aware of wounds and brokenness; filled with the painful knowledge that God knows the sinful condition of our lives, aware of our human limitations and inadequacies, yet we still dare to come and share in the love feast presented before us by the Creator God, our all-forgiving host.

This simple yet profound parable of God's kingdom has some important theological implications that may enable congregations to learn how to invite, welcome, and accept all who wish to enter the church, regardless of their abilities or limitations. To begin with, we need to remember that the good news of this story is that the invitation to God's banquet table is not based upon our human good works, nor dependent upon our money and fame. Instead, the invitation to this banquet is the gift of salvation extended through God's gift of grace. We are invited because God first loved us. The only way one can remain outside and away from the banquet is by consciously turning down the invitation. The New Testament theologian Joseph Fitzmyer writes, while we cannot save ourselves, we can very well damn ourselves.[8]

This idea of grace runs contrary to the implied message of the scarcity paradigm suggesting that love and attention are limited resources. The scarcity paradigm is overtly and covertly communicated to many disabled people and their families. Many leaders in congregations determine whether a disabled person may attend worship or other activities by asking the narrow question, "What can they *do* in worship?" As if God values us only for what we can do, not for who we are.

Nowhere in scriptures is it written that one has to be able to *do* certain things in order to worship God, or that one must have a specific I.Q., or behave in a socially appropriate fashion. It has been said by many who worship with those who have been labeled severely or profoundly mentally retarded that the greatest gift they give is the understanding that God values and enjoys *who* we are, as a child of God's, rather than what we *do*. What one finally gets out of worship is, most likely, something between the "invited guest" and the "host" of the banquet.

Another important lesson is the realization that God's banquet table is big enough for all who were invited to sit at it and enjoy the meal. There is no sense in the parable that the banquet room was not big enough or overcrowded. There was so much space left over at one point that the servant was sent out a second time to bring in more people. Each person has a special place at God's table at this love feast. No one is turned away from the feast.

This lesson from God's banquet table runs contrary to some congregations, which may imitate a family reunion. When I grew up, dinners at family reunions were in two rooms. In the dining room was the adult table, with china, crystal, the best silver on Irish linen tablecloth, with a floral bouquet and candles in the center. Meanwhile, in the kitchen was the room for the children on a rickety card table, folding chairs, plasticware for eating with, and no flowers. This room was childproof.

Many churches have opted for this family reunion paradigm for worship. Some churches have set aside a separate chapel, sometimes called the "weeping chapel," located off of the main sanctuary for those with disabilities to sit in, along with nursing mothers and their crying, babbling babies. Others, like those with a hearing impairment, are tired of feeling closed out of the hearing-centered parish during worship and have established their own churches for the "deaf community" in their denominations. This parable raises a question for our churches: Is this banquet table symbolic of our gathering, willing to welcome all who wish to enter?

The final lesson is remembering that all persons who were invited and came to the banquet had this one, essential characteristic in common: they probably had never seen themselves as members of a community of love. All persons have seen themselves as disconnected individuals, with long-forgotten family connections, isolated from the Jewish community. They were hiding in the alleyways because they were lonely outcasts.

Being brought together through the host's gracious invitation, gathered around a common table, they began to see that they were more or less like the other invited guests: they saw other poor strangers transformed, unexpectedly, into invited, honored guests. Who would have thought that the one with leprosy, the outlaw, the disenfranchised, the undervalued, would be God's welcomed guest? All it took was accepting the invitation to come to God's feast.

What is moving in this story is that not one of these people could ever repay the host in kind, for none of these individuals had ever tasted or seen such splendor as was found at this feast. They simply accepted God's invitation to "taste my banquet." And in accepting this invitation, their lives were forever changed.

The challenge for the church is to break away from the dominant culture's misperceptions that keep those who have a disabling condition on the disenfranchised, undervalued margins of society. Jesus' parable establishes a vision of God's kingdom that gives those who are disabled a place not only close to God's heart in God's kingdom, but more important, the realization that the one with a disabling condition has an invaluable place in the living body of Christ. But Jesus' parable calls for nothing less than a conversion of the church's collective heart in inviting and welcoming all who wish to worship God. To God, people with disabling conditions are not just another social action project for our churches. This is not social posturing; this is kingdom-of-God ethics ruling:[9] people who have some real limitations and unique gifts, invited to have a seat at the finest meal at God's love feast.

The reason why Jesus told the parable is so that we have a practical, concrete vision of the loving nature of God's kingdom in our churches. Such love, writes the social critic Wendell Berry, is never abstract: "It does not adhere to the universe of the planet or the nation or the institution or the profession, but to the singular sparrows of the street, the lilies of the field, 'the least of these my brothers and sisters.'"[10]

Jesus is calling the church to live its life according to this alternative vision of God's kingdom. We are to move over in the pews and discover that God wants all who wish to enter our sanctuaries to worship God to be free to do so. Christ's body is made up of those who think they are able and those whom we have labeled "disabled," who appear less fortunate, broken, and wounded. We need these "unexpected guests" to be invited in order to be reminded that it is God in Christ alone who can heal the wounds deep within, and mend the broken heart, because we are God's children. God's banquet table is a place for all Christians, upholding the common good of all members of Christ's body, on earth as it is in heaven.

7

Lost Pilgrims
in an Alien Land

The theologian Stanley Hauerwas writes that our life stories reveal our character, which is also a reflection of the community in which our faith is shaped and nurtured.[1] The truth of this statement is manifested in the following stories of three young people. These stories tell us much about their character and reveal also essential fragments of the Christian and Jewish communities' sacred story in which they were raised. These young people are residents of a hospital for disabled children and adolescents. They are the ones who, quietly or defiantly, tell us that they are leaving home, are using drugs, or are escaping to the violence of the inner-city streets. The children and adolescents come from across the country, from African-American and Hispanic-American families of different configurations, many raised by extended family members. Some are from wealthy families and many from lower-income backgrounds. The one thing these children and adolescents have in common in this institution is that they are all labeled and categorized with a disabling condition: they have behavioral disorders.

Ben

The first narrative is Ben's.[2] Ben is an energetic, lanky and tall fifteen-year-old adolescent who is Jewish, having already participated in the bar mitzvah ritual in his home synagogue. I met Ben soon after I came to the hospital and introduced myself as the Director of Religious Life. He beckoned to me after that first meeting to come to his room. Sitting on his bed in his room, he got up on a chair and started throwing books at me, which would help me in getting to know him. The first book he threw at me was *Catcher in the Rye* by J.D. Salinger, saying "Now you know my hero!" The second book was *The Diary of Anne Frank*, "Now you know what my faith is." The third book was Walt Whitman's *Leaves of Grass*, saying "Now you know what I like to do."

Since that first meeting, our relationship has been one of mentor and disciple, while at times I am scribe to his poetry writing. He will often come into my office and dictate his poetry while rocking wildly to and fro in the rocking chair at first, then slowing down to a gentle rock. In his poetry he is trying to tell me what has been happening in the care unit; he depicts for me his relationships at home, and is revealing much about his relationship with God.

For example, one of the first poems was "The Day Will Come":

> The day will come
> When we will all realize
> What fools we've been
>   and stop these foolish lies,
> And come to our senses and reach for God's hand.
> And until then we will be imperfect people
>   in an imperfect land.

"There," he said, thrusting the poem under my nose. "What do you think? You probably don't like it." I told him I was struck by the truth of the poem. He smiled. Then I asked him to interpret his poem for me. "We're ruining this world that God made. And He's probably none too happy about it . . . or with us. That's what I think." With that, he got up from my rocking chair, and over we went to the care unit.

Around Thanksgiving, I asked him to write a poem for the holiday. This is the poem which revealed more of his theology:

> Give thanks to God
>   And your answered prayers.
> Give thanks to your fulfilled dreams
>   That didn't turn into nightmares.
> Give thanks to that hope

That helped fulfill your dreams,
Even when it was coming undone by the seams.
Give thanks to the people
Who helped you to reach that star.
But don't forget that strength and courage
You had when your goals seemed so far.

Glenn

The second narrative belongs to thirteen-year-old Glenn who has blond hair, blue eyes, and a quiet, gentle spirit. There is nothing violent in his demeanor. Telling me about life in the care unit, it appears that he is a keen observer of life, watching and listening to his peers, letting them teach him about life as he learned from his two older brothers outside the institution.

Glenn and I have recently begun meeting on a weekly basis to talk about God and life. Sometimes we meet in his room, other times in my office, and he asks me about God. He believes in God, knowing that God is here, acknowledging that it is God who has pulled him through some frightful moments of life in dealing with a drug habit forced upon him by one of his parents at an early age.

His interest in God and the church was sparked during his time in a home for "troubled boys," which was connected to a monastery and abbey near his hometown. He remembers the ornateness of the church, with a larger than life cross of the crucified Christ in the front of the sanctuary. He and his friends would run around the church in the still of night, searching for leftover wine, playing among the confessional booths, hiding in the pews in a darkened sanctuary, and daring one another to drink the holy water.

Besides running around with his friends, certain rituals of the church have made an indelible impression upon this young man. For example, when we talked about God, his image of God is that of spirit, a loving spirit "that surrounds and keeps all of us safe." In drawing a picture of his impression of Jesus for me, he drew an image of Jesus with a halo over his head and a crown upon his head, because he has heard of Jesus being referred to as "the King of Kings and Lord of Lords, or something like that," he says.

Glenn comes up with many questions that would challenge many theologians in academe, querying me about the nature of God, the rituals of the church, and issues of life and death. Glenn says he knows that God is here because of the love the staff shows to him and others.

Glenn believes in the power of God's love and desire to answer prayers because of his experiences in jails and detention centers. He remembered one cold, January night, when he was nine years old, and he had gone to night court because the police found him in possession of illegal drugs:

> I prayed to Jesus when I go to court over drugs. I didn't want to be put in jail. My Mom met me at the court house. We rode together in the cop car. I prayed that Jesus would save me from jail. But I went [there] anyway. And I was OK. I think with Jesus you have to meet him halfway. He comes part of the way in answering your prayers, but you've got to meet him and do some things for him as well. That's the way it works. You got to meet Jesus as well . . . halfway.

Stephanie

The third narrative is Stephanie's, a young African-American woman who attends a Baptist church when she's at home, who loves to sing and write poetry to God, like the character "Celie" in Alice Walker's novel *The Color Purple*. Our relationship began when she found out that I was reading Ben's poetry. "I'm a poet, too. Aren't I good enough for you?" she asked one day, smiling, knowing that this bait would hook me.

When asked what she liked about church, she said that she loved to go to church because of the community:

> What I like about church is going and clapping hands. If someone says something good, then we may say "Thank you," real proper like, or else some really get into it, saying "Amen . . . Alleluia." I like that. I feel like standing up and sayin' that sometimes myself.
>
> For me, church is a place you can go to, and once, when you're in problems outside [in the world], and you can come in and get a peace of mind, and feeling like rejoicing and stuff.

The only thing that Stephanie does not like about church is the offering, which they do more than once during worship in her church. "They's always going for money it seems."

Stephanie's image of God is as the Father of Jesus, a merciful God who is always there for his people:

> You can curse God, and God is still there; you are already saved in his name. God is very selfish because he wants you for himself. But because he want you he is very forgiving if you ask for forgiveness. That's all you have to do is ask God for forgiveness.
>
> I know God because I speak in tongues. God gives me a warm feeling in my heart. [And when] my heart is warm, then my hands get wet, and I gotta walk around . . . gotta scream and holler . . . got to say "Alleluia!" My mama said that when that happens, that's when the Holy Ghost is inside you . . . you feel something.

What she likes about God is the promise: "That if you walk in his word, you'll have everlasting life; that's pretty cool . . . forgiving people. God's a pretty cool dude. My mama don't like me using that language, but he is."

One day while attending a group therapy session, Stephanie shared with the group this poem, meant for me:

> Come unto me all ye that labor and I will give you rest.
> Someone who says they are God.
> How do I know someone named Jesus and God ever lived?
> Could there possibly have been a man who turned water
>   into wine?
> People worship him and so-call "drink his blood."
> WHY?
> Only one man.
> If he was living, he'd be a millionaire.
> Mr. God, help me if you are so mighty and powerful!
> Or is it that you only help people who give money
>   to the churches,
> With fake preachers who has a cold beer after services?

"I mean every word of this poem," she said. A theologian in search of God.

Faith in Search of Understanding

What emerges in listening to these insightful narratives and the questions being asked, participating in the ongoing dialogue throughout the days of working with these adolescents, are stories that reveal the wonderfully diverse character of faith. In their stories about life, God, Jesus, the church, and religion, the reader becomes aware that this is truly faith in search of understanding. From among the stories told, each one of these young people is asking me, or more important asking God, to help make sense of the world that is often more chaos than cosmos, more helter-skelter than controlled and predictable. Ben is claiming that until we come to our senses and reach out to God, we will have to work together, holding hands as imperfect people in an imperfect land. Glenn is asking questions about the church and God, trusting that he can pursue these questions because God in Christ has answered his prayers before, helping him survive jail and rides in police cars as a nine-year-old child. Stephanie, strong in her opinions of church life, asks questions about the nature of God amid seeming injustices in her world. In other words, these young people are doing and being theological: they are asking important, complex questions about the nature of God's relationship with humankind in sophisticated, and sometimes not-so-sophisticated ways. They are trying to understand what is happening in their community and life experiences as part of their journey of faith.

Where do these questions and religious narratives fit within the medical and psychological models of the institutions where they live, play, and study? Like other settings for children and adolescents with behavioral disorders, most of the secular institutions have focused primarily on the body and the mind of these young people, but not on the spirit. The very definitions used to describe what is occurring in a young person's life who is outwardly and overtly disturbed or agitated serves different professional and scientific purposes, and reflects diverse perspectives as all definitions of disabling conditions are social constructions. In terms of treating a behavioral disorder as an issue of the body or neurological disorder, the medical and psychiatric field may view a behavioral disorder as stemming from an organic dysfunction needing psychopharmacological treatments.[3]

A behavioral disorder may be viewed as an issue of the mind or psyche. Many in psychology believe that human life is a challenge to our power to shape someone else's life to the greater society's purposes.[4] With this philosophy, psychologists have described behavior disorders as psychological in nature to the extent that a child's behavior deviates from a relative social norm, occurring with a frequency or intensity that is judged to be abnormal. In psychology, many choose to work with young people with behavioral disorders using primarily behavior modification techniques and programs in controlling and modifying a young child's behavior.[5]

While the medical and psychological perspectives focus on the disabling condition, "behavior disorder," as a dysfunction of body and mind, neither field has adequately addressed the issue of spirit. Yet it is the spirit or, in the language of the Jewish and Christian communities, the faith of these young people that is longing to be heard and is awaiting a response from others who believe in God. The journey of faith of these young people, a journey that began before they came to the institution, needs to be nurtured again and given direction. For those who are Christians, the body of Christ is uniquely crafted and empowered by God's love as the compassionate community, able to answer the call and questions of these young people. While the medical, psychological, and educational fields are trying to help these adolescents, nonetheless, questions of God continue to arise, unanswered or not taken seriously. Many of these young people wonder if God is truly listening to their voices. These young people are singing songs of lament to God as lost pilgrims in an alien land.

How are we in our communities of faith to understand and appreciate such provocative questions about God's presence? Do we realize that these young people are lost pilgrims in our modern, secular society? These are pilgrims who have left behind them the often fractured security of their home, friends, and burnt-out neighborhoods. For some, they left with little choice about the situation. Many young people in specialized hospitals are there because they were sexually, physically, or psychologically abused at home. For others, their families no longer knew how to cope with the sometimes erratic behavior of the young child or teen. A few leave a place of drugs and sleepless nights filled with the dark violence of the streets. Said one young man from the streets of an urban environment, "I'm afraid that Jesus won't forgive me for my sins. I'm afraid the acts have been so bad that Jesus won't forgive me. If he don't, I don't know what I'll do in this world once I'm away from this place."

These young people, bereft of home, friends, school, and church, are metaphorically standing in the middle of the public square of our world stuck, naked, lost, lonely, violated, and vulnerable. And they are scared. Scared because they have been taken out of the world of the threatening known into a place that is unknown, temporary, and, at first, even more threatening. Not trusting in others, they know not where to hide. They are like John Bunyan's pilgrim, Christian, with a heavy burden on their back, individually crying to the world, "What shall I do?" in the City of Destruction.[6]

Yet while standing naked and alone as individuals in the public square, they each sing their song of lament. For while they miss their homes, friends, and families, they know there is another place for them, though they do not know how to get there, or where they are necessarily headed. The goal of their life journey has not become visible or concrete. In their questions to God about life, these young people, exiled from their homes and the familiarity of the known, sing a song of lamentation. Echoing the words of Psalm 137, they are singing about their need for community, lamenting that which has been taken away from them, and dreading the isolation where they are. While living in a foreign land like a hospital, they are like the Israelites who remember something of God and Zion: "By the rivers of Babylon, there we sat down, and there we wept, when we remembered Zion. On the willows there we hung up our harps" (Psalm 137:1,2, NRSV). The adolescents, though they spent only a few short days of their lives in their respective Christian or Jewish community, are like the children of Israel as they remember those days when they seemed to be closer to God when living with their family and friends.

What the young people yearn for is movement from this place of isolation, loneliness, and disconnectedness, to some clear destination, some place with people who care for them. They long to be healed as their spirit is in disarray; they wish to reorder the state of psychological and spiritual confusion, which springs out of the core of their being and infects the rest of life. So strong is this confusion that it is contagious, influencing the lives of family members, friends, staff, and acquaintances.[7]

To move these young people on in their journey of faith, they need to worship in a community of believers, to be in a sacred gathering where the manifestation of divine action has occurred time and again. They are like the children of Israel who would travel to holy places to worship Yahweh during passover (Luke 2:41). They are like Chaucer's medieval pilgrims, simple people, who traveled from the ends of every shire in England, "to see the holy, blissful martyr [St. Thomas a Becket], who helped them when they were sick."[8] Like the pilgrims of old, these young people are asking us to be the community of the faithful where they may go to ask their questions. For in the company of believers they may truly experience God's compassionate healing.

To guide these young people on, church members need to be co-pilgrims with these young people, guiding them along the way of the sacred story learned in Christian communities and lived out in the world. As co-pilgrim, the task is to share and walk with them, to be the good companion who does not abandon the pilgrim, even in the face of great temptations and death, like the friend "Faithful" to Bunyan's pilgrim, Christian.[9] As companion, church members are to be present as storytellers, retelling the sacred story because the sacred story is the map for life's journey.[10] For it is in the sacred story of God's love, recorded in Scripture, and the telling of God's story, that one discovers and unleashes the reservoir of God's gift of faith, hope, and love that alone can heal, nurture, and guide these young people's spirits in disarray.

The sacred story of the Christian community creates an atmosphere in which truth becomes discernable as a pattern.[11] Truth, love, care, compassion can be understood only in the context of story. Outside story, these concepts become one-dimensional and lose their vitality and relevance. For these concepts are alive yet unpronounceable. They are known only in the act of living the truth of God's love.

Along with the power of the story is the art of storytelling. The writer Barry Lopez writes that the act of storytelling:

> [Involves] the skillful invocation of unimpeachable sources and a listener's knowledge that no hypocrisy or subterfuge is involved . . . the intent of the storyteller, then, must be to evoke, honestly, some single aspect of all that [the story] contains. The storyteller knows that because different individuals grasp the story at different levels, the focus of his regard for truth must be at the primary one—with who was there, what happened, when, where, and why things occurred. It is then possible for the story to be more successful than the storyteller himself is able to imagine.[12]

The truth of God's love is most powerfully revealed in the sacred story of the Bible. It is in the telling and retelling of the story, the singing, the acting out, and painting of the sacred story, that the message of God's love for humankind and creation is made clear and tangible. The final destination of the pilgrimage is apparent, and the pilgrim moves toward a place of deep healing, where the fractured wounds of callous disregard are healed with a new heart, and the spirit is at rest.

Perplexed Pilgrims

The young people who have been diagnosed as "behavior disorders" are lost pilgrims in an alien land. It is important to note that they are not new to God's story, for they are able to describe God and God's nature in ways that reveal a faith that is alive. They are waiting for someone, somewhere, to accompany them on the journey and point out to them that sacred place where they can find rest for their souls and answers to their queries of God. In their search for healing, God, through the body of Christ, has created a place and a people in which their state of psychological and spiritual confusion in relationship with others may be healed. These young people are calling those who know God and the path to that sacred place to walk with them for they cannot make it on their own much longer.

What is miraculous in these stories is that these children are telling and living out their interpretation of the sacred story amid a secular institution where, before the presence of a Presbyterian pastor, no one was at liberty to talk about God, let alone engage in theological inquiry. Few of the young people have been to a church or synagogue since they came to the institution five to eighteen months ago. For some, they did not think much about God and Jesus until they were thrust individually into this temporary, alien setting. Yet somewhere, somehow, the stories of God's love, Jesus' faithfulness, and the Holy Spirit's peace has made an indelible impression upon the hearts and minds of these young people. The ideas and dreams stirred by the sacred story have survived and flourished amid an arid land. They remember the stories of Zion amid their isolation.

The gift that many young people with a behavior disorder have for the church is that of telling the truth. Among professionals who work with such young people, there is the sense that if these adolescents sense the therapist's weakness or "Achilles' heel" in working with them, they will exploit it to their advantage whenever possible. Often the professional tries to maintain a facade of strength and professionality, placing on themselves a mask of knowledge and competence to hide fear and insecurity.

The "weakness" in others that these young people are very sensitive to is the sense of incongruity between the truths of God's sacred story and the contradictory actions of those who say they believe in God. Having come out of lives riddled with stories that were filled with lies, hidden truths, and abuse, creating a dark void of trust in their lives, the young people know when someone is or is not telling and living the truth. While the rest of us forget what we see and forget what we *do not* see around us, a form of socialized blindness where we overlook the incongruities and subtle lies of life, such blindness among these young people has not been socialized yet.[13] They upset us because they turn the bright lights of truth upon our hidden, dark lies, demanding honesty from us. They validate, in their own way, that which we all see or do not see. They remove the shadows in our darkened caves. These lost pilgrims, whether in their raging anger or depressive, audible silence, are calling for direction to Zion. They are calling for us to give them our hand and walk with them as co-pilgrims in the journey of faith.

• • •

The following four chapters are the spiritual narratives of the three young people introduced in this chapter. There is Ben, the young Jewish poet; Glenn, a closet Baltimore Oriole fan; and Stephanie, a sassy young woman who lives to question God.

8

A Poet Among Us

In the journey of faith, Jews and Christians alike have a need to share both life's joys as well as its struggles among a community of believers. In sharing their experiences, the Old Testament theologian Bernhard Anderson wrote that God's people quickly discovered that the goal of their journey was not going to be reached by an easy highway: "instead, they must take the roundabout way, the detour into 'the wasteland' [T. S. Eliot] which poets and artists have portrayed."[1]

One rich and powerful source of loving guidance and support for people in either ecstatic bliss or trial has been the book of Psalms. For the Psalms have enabled people to express their concerns and needs to the Almighty out of the depths of their hurt as well as in moments of high praise to Yahweh.

The Old Testament scholar Claus Westermann described the Psalms as "prayed poetry," since the Psalms were meant to be sung and recited to musical tunes. The Psalms capture the language that the worshiping community uses for talking to and about God, in response to the Almighty's presence in their collective life.

In working at this hospital, I have found some poets who are writing their own psalms, creating poems that express their joy in knowing that there *is* a God even amid the chaos of a psychiatric facility. The poems also become a way of describing or giving voice to the bleakness of life when all of life is colored in shades of gray. These young poets depend upon their gift as a way of communicating the essence of their journey.

Ben is such a poet among us at this hospital. He has captured the bittersweetness of this life of faith. For a year, Ben and I talked about two things: poetry and God, and usually poetry *about* God. In one of our first conversations, we talked mainly about God:

> God is everywhere, not necessarily kept in one place. He is in the air, in the wall, the earth we walk on, everywhere. Or God is a body, yeah, like this is probably his leg . . . it kind of smells don't you think? And this is his hairy body. No . . . I've got it: we're a cell in God, the earth is a cell in the large body of God, and we're floating, right? Get this picture: we're just floating in the body of God.
>
> [But sometimes] God isn't here . . . he get's you going, and then he leaves. [Like in the] Holocaust. Like a bird, coming along and feeding the small birds with food it has collected, and then one day, the bird pushes the baby chick out. God gives you what you need, like the mother bird, feeding you, and then pushes you out one day, whether you like it or not, whether you're ready or not.
>
> God's love is all over the place, all around. In the air we breathe, in the walls, the water. God's all over the place.

After our first meeting, we rarely had such revealing talks about God. Instead, what followed was pure poetry as Ben wrote what communicated both the pains of living in an institution as well as the fear of returning home. His poems, like that of the Psalmist, also danced between praise and thanksgiving to God, as well as angry defiance and abject horror at the thought that he may have been left alone by God, utterly naked and vulnerable to the world of the psychiatric profession.

In the following pages are bits and pieces of Ben's poetry, as well as descriptions of the almost manic mood swings that Ben would get into during his stay at this institution. For Ben, poetry was not only his way to escape, but often his way to express his perspective of the world around him creatively, as it is for many adolescents. As was mentioned earlier, he would come into my office, sit down in the office rocking chair, and wildly rock to and fro as if he were on a wild bucking stallion, and then slow down to a nice "trot." While first rocking, he would tell me all the things that were *not* going his way on the unit, with his social worker, the psychiatrist, the other young people on the unit, and his family.

Then I would hand him a pad of legal paper, a pencil that was recently sharpened, and let him write as one of the resident poets among us at the hospital. I would sit at the computer as his scribe, waiting to transcribe what he would write down and reveal publicly: the private, poetic images dancing in his head. He misspelled many of the words in the poems, and his poems have their own unique pattern. What follows are some of the dancing poetic images in this young man's life, shared during the many conversations we would have in my office. The poems are composed by a young man who was and is on a journey to find a resting place for his troubled and disturbed soul—a soul of unrest.

DAYDREAM

As I sit and stare
And watch you over there,
It makes me wonder why,
As I sit here in the rye,
If wishes do come true,
Why can't I be with you?
And if dreams are real,
Why won't my heart heal?
Why don't I feel the need to see my answers answered correctly,
And why try to perfect imperfection?

DAYDREAM, TOO

Once upon a dream
In a land I call my own,
I had a talk with my conscience
In a quiet sort of tone.
Not about the future,
But all about the past.
It told me if changes weren't made,
I surely would not last.
So now I see the world from the outside in,
        not the inside out.
And now I see the world,
        and some of what it's all about.

DAYDREAM, ALSO

You are born to live,
And you live to die.

Your emotions are there,
It's up to you to cry.
Your conscience is there,
It's your choice to lie.
Hate in you is there,
It's up to you to love.
The choice to be under is there,
It's your choice to stay above.
It's your choice to make the move smart.
Play it safe . . . listen to your heart.

SOCIETY

Society:
Life in such variety,
Cultures by the pound,
With so many new waves,
We're lucky we don't drown.
With conflict so great,
We're lucky to still be around.
And then when it comes back,
To the simple pleasures in life,
We're six feet underground.

BEN

I tried to cool the world
With warmth, love and care,
But with time it proves to be too hot,
        for human hands to bare.

I had a talk with God,
And together we conversed,
And agreed, as you will read,
That this is not the worst:

Time is guilty of its past,
With the present as its alibi,
The future as its lawyer,

I think no one will try,
To persecute execute the ones who stand before,
I say with no excuse,
"What's the use?"
And further write no more.

LIFE I

A day when the young were bold,
And the old were wise,
When the earth was cold and in disguise.
When love prospered in various ways:
Oh, those were the days.

In a day when men fought to live,
And women in black had stories to give,
When the sun shown down its rays:
Oh, those were the days.

When life had to fulfill its own meanings,
And the land shown off its greenings.
And hope had its own screenings,
Although my theories grown its grays
I still say:
Oh, those were the days.

LIFE III

A light from heaven gives me the will,
The will to live and go on still,
And though that will revives my hope,
The continuing pressure is still mine to cope.
While I deal with this over here,
There's still that over there.
Don't expect both our loads for me to bear,
Or maybe we can share?

LIFE IV

When the day is gone,
And the night has been and past,

I see the world through different eyes,
And watch it spin so fast.
And then I see a shadow cast,
Thus knowing the future is at hand,
And look back and wonder how long
this bitterness will last?

December 9th

Today, when I came on the unit, Ben was bouncing his basketball on the floor and sometimes against the walls of his bedroom, swearing at his social worker because she was not paying enough attention to *his* problems. He kept on muttering to himself, loud enough for me to hear: "They're out to get me," over and over again.

When I asked Ben to go out and play some basketball with me, a game of H-O-R-S-E, he agreed, still muttering, saying now that his roommate better not touch his cassette tape machine.

Out on the basketball court, he kept on talking about how much he hated the social worker, and that he wanted a replacement. He continued to talk down the rest of the staff, saying that they were out to "get me. They want to get me down a level or two because I'm close to being discharged, and they want to persecute me." Throughout the whole time, he made every basket, and I lost the game of H-O-R-S-E.

THE LIGHT FOR YOU AND I

When life seems its worst,
When your broken heart seems ready to burst,
When hope seems to be cursed,
I'll look north in search of you.
For the day to change
        those times are few.
South, north, east, or west,
The devil holds me captive
        in the darkness of his chest.
And though I pray to God before I die,
The light so far for you and I.

REALITY

I had friends.
I had companionship.

I thought?

And then again, I wanted to think.
They say each day a star is born.
That is only fact.
That is only half.

Each day a star dies.

You see, the human race is nothing but anti-reality;
Mere sociopaths we are.
It's only a matter of us who see through open eyes.
Not all killers in this race of ours,
But mainly actors,
   mere performers on a colossal stage,
   in the middle of the universe,
   in the middle of society.
A society of love, hope, and dreams;
A society for mind wanderers wonders;
Of hopes, dreams, and lovers.
A place for actors.
An uncontrollable script
   called the past, present, and future.
And is our subconscious really conscious?
Or viceversa?
Has our destiny been set in stone?
Or is it all unknown
   to those who are blind?

IGNORING VOICES

I try to ignore the voices
But they pound my aching head.
With such enormous force
The black wolf's being fed,
The hungry, angry, thirsty beast.

Is there no in-between?

He's making my conscience his Thanksgiving feast.
Leave my soul at rest,
Put the white wolf to the test.
I promise I will not fail,
I'll win this fight yet,
Without the wall of betrayal.

January 9th

Ben pointed at me across the campus today, indicating that he wanted to talk to me today. Later in the day, I came over to the unit, and he waltzed out of his room, grabbed my keys out of my hand, unlocked the double locked doors, and off we went to my office.

For the first few minutes he played at my computer, running letters together in hopes of making a design. He had been home recently, and had seen the film *Father of the Bride*, which he liked.

I asked him to draw some pictures for me. When I asked him to draw a picture of God, he threw the paper back at me, saying "You just can't draw God. When will you get the point?"

When I asked him to draw love, he threw the paper at me again, saying in a matter-of-fact tone of voice, "You can't freely draw that which is only felt and experienced between two people. Love is all around you; you can't see it because it is everywhere you are. It is so large you can't see it for what it really is."

TURNING THE TIDE

When the tides begin to turn,
When the game goes its own way,
'Tis when my blood begins to yearn
    for a new manipulative game to play.

And though the web might get thick quick,
And ponders of a spider's trick,
And when the dew falls thick upon
    the silky strands the threads of dawn.
And though the trap might be revealed,
The thoughts of mine are still concealed.

March 11th

Ben asked me to come to his room. We begin talking about his leaving the hospital. He thanked me for believing in him enough so that he had a chance to write and read poetry. He said that when we had met, he had hit the bottom of his own experiences here. However, since that time, we have been talking about his poetry, and he has felt better, and is starting to feel good about himself and what he can do. He has begun to write more and more poetry, and that has made a difference in his life.

TIME IS . . .

Time is a joker in disguise.
Time is a prophet unseen.
Time is a devil or of God.
Time is loving.
Time is mean.
Time is of the essence.
Time is in our presence.
Time is you,
  is what to do,
  is what you do.

April 6th

The following poems were written when Ben was on unit restrictions for one kind of mischief and another. He has not been permitted to come off the unit for some time, and he is truly depressed. Because of his "captivity," most of the following poems contain the themes of breaking out, liberation, and sadness.

BREAKABLE LOCKS

The signs of time and turning pages,
History reveals its locked up ages,
While people act on secret stages,
Some history might still be hidden,
But by far, it's not forbidden.

I pray I'm not the one
      to leave my lock undone.

CONFUSION

If destiny or fate from fault
Could bring life to a sudden halt,
If petty lives could really change,
Why do I feel so cold and strange?

And if I can't avoid abuse,
I say, "What's the use?"

If life is death just waiting to die,
Or is this world just one big lie?
Or is it just an answer I long for?
Or should I ask for more?
Or am I just not sure?

UP

When the day comes to a close,
Nobody but me knows
      that I'll survive another day,
      somehow I'll find a way.
I made it once,
So this should be no exception,
For I know my life's direction.

WHERE'S THE PLACE FOR ME?

When my throat is tight,
and there's no guiding light,
I look unto the west,
And challenge up the best,
When time turns against me,
And there's no light to see,

I wonder of a place that's free,
That's just the place for me?

The Love that Got All Wet

For the kindness you have brought,
For the love and caring thought,
For the times that we went through,
The laughter after me and you.
Walking, talking, holding hands,
All across the open sands.

So when the day came around,
Without a worry ever found,
You made that awful sound,
"Will you marry me?"

My damn face hit the ground,
I put it so profound,
Possibly, a bit too much sound?
Because every living thing around me,
Knew that I had made a mistake.
"What have I done, for goodness sake?"
But now I may regret,
The love that got all wet.

Storms

When I feel the storm
        creeping up behind,
I turn around,
Without a sound,
And look it in the eye.

My friends, they follow my lead,
And stop to join the stare,
And turn with every care,

To face a forming nightmare,
And dodge the doom of dare.

SECURITY

Secure the locks that bond our love.
Secure the heavens up above.
Secure the peace throughout the world;
Secure my faith and harmony
   that brought the moral life in me.

Secure the things that give me strength and will,
   that keeps my world so warm and still.

Secure the sun that lights my way,
   through and through each and every day.

I thank my family and closest ones
   for they are to me inner suns.

I pray to God to keep me safe,
   because this is what makes my faith.

FIND PEACE

As I try to find peace,
In a world of war.
As I search for sanity,
Where there is no more.

And even if the fools of this world
   who shape our society
    cannot see the meaning in my work;
For all God's grace,
Let Him guide me to a better place.

June 25th

 Ben was in a overdramatic mood today. When I went into his room at first, he was not sure that he wanted to talk with me, saying that I should feel guilty for his being in this place. He is mad at everyone and anyone. At one point, he is yelling about the hospital staff who say that they want him to go home with his family, "but then they keep me away from them." The next minute, he is swearing and cursing about his family, saying that they do not want him and they are ruining him. He is picking up all sizes of boxes and throwing them around the room, but none come near me.

For the last few months he has been on a new program, with the goal of his going home. But now there is talk of another program, or extending this program a bit longer, and Ben is not amused, getting so close to me that he is spitting his words out, and the spit hits me in the face. He is angrily pacing as he delivers his Joblike plea for answers to his questions of the future:

> Why are they doing this to me? Do they like to drive people crazy? And where the _____ is God in all of this? Doesn't God care? And where is Jesus when you need him? Where the _____ is your God? We're shitting on this world that we have, and God isn't going to do a damn thing, is He? What kind of loving God is this that won't save us from ourselves?

August 11th

Ben is leaving this institution for a step-down facility which is more like a halfway home tomorrow. We go out to see a movie, *A Stranger Among Us*, a different kind of "cops and robber" movie, where a Gentile, female police officer is working in the context of a Hasidic Jewish community in New York City. Ben, being Jewish in a largely Christian institutional culture, can relate to the "stranger" in the film.

As we go out to a fast-food restaurant after the movie, he tells me that he is going to miss me and quite a few of the people at the hospital, including the social worker, but not the psychiatrist and some of the nurses. He is amused that he is *actually* going to miss someone, anyone, from this hospital, which he has hated with such relish in the last few years that he has been here.

Ben's life is a question mark to be placed against Ben's experiences of life. Like those who wrote the Psalms, there are glimpses of both great joy and gladdened exultation of God, as well as moments of deep pain and utter angst. There is no single, absolute answer, yet, to Ben's questions of life. For with Ben, while one answer works for him one day, the question changes the next day, if not the next minute, and the old answer just does not work for him anymore. And yet, even in the midst of the questions upon questions, there is a stubborn faith that is born out through it all, and Ben still acknowledges the presence of God.

I end this chapter of Ben's poetry with a poem that questions life:

LIFE

Life . . .
You call this living?
You should check your analogy.
You call this living in your so-called society?
Examine . . . review . . . try it again.

Sorry, but life is a pain.
And the world is one outlet,
A host to a race of infinity.
Will we live to see eternity?

9

Finding God in Motley Crue

One of the constant questions throughout this book has to do with the emergence of our knowing that we are in a faithful relationship with God: How do we know God? And how is God made known to us? These questions have been of central concern to congregations and parishes, pastors and priests, and all of God's people throughout the church's history.

Most often, we try hard to strategically arrange our lives, our friendships, our commitments, our churches, our worship spaces, our educational programs, our pastoral therapeutic interventions, and (with fingers crossed for good luck and good measure) we hope that something we have done will ignite and infuse the epiphany moments when we clearly know God has come to be with us and be known to us in concrete fashion.

The naturalist Annie Dillard writes about such false hopes and good intentions in trying to predict and control God's presence in our midst during worship in her book *Holy the Firm*:

> I often think of the set pieces of liturgy as certain words which people have successfully addressed to God without their getting killed. In the high churches they saunter through the liturgy like Mohawks along a strand of scaffolding who have long since forgotten their danger. If God were to blast such a service to bits, the congregation would be, I believe, genuinely shocked. But the low churches, you expect it any minute. This is the beginning of wisdom.[1]

Therefore, despite our best intentions and efforts in controlling

God's presence and passage through human time and our humble abodes, making God safe for human consumption, God has always been creative in making God known, be it in the midst of a burning bush, the still small voice out of rushing wind, or in the incarnation of a baby child born to poor parents in a dirty stable for animals, not humans, in Bethlehem. As the theologian Stanley Hauerwas has often said, God will not be domesticated by us. There is a wildness about God; a lovingly exciting, yet exasperating unpredictable quality about God's unpronounced presence and action in our life that is good for us. For it reminds us that we are not in control of our lives after all. God is the one who is in control.

God *continues* to be creative in making God known to humankind, even among children with behavioral and emotional disabilities. Take my friend Glenn, a young boy who spent time in this hospital because of his drug problem and bouts of deep, seemingly unending, depression. In our relationship I have learned, once again, not to be surprised about how God is known to us. For Glenn came to know God through, of all things, heavy metal music, that "tool of the devil," a "contraband item" in the hospital culture, which is usually confiscated by the staff. More precisely, Glenn came to truly believe in God after hearing the song "Shout at the Devil!" by the group Motley Crue, a heavy metal group that he dreams about being a singer for in his life.

Before finding out about Glenn's experience of God in listening to Motley Crue, it is important to understand the significance of Glenn's knowing God. For Glenn's relationship with God began on his journey through the dizzying maze of mental health services.

On the surface of life, Glenn appears to be a normal, average teenager, with many of the same likes and dislikes as peers his same age. For example, he has a "thing" for cars, especially fast, imported European cars like Porsche and Lotus: "The Lotus looks wild, and it costs around $80,000 to $90,000." There is a large poster of a red Lotus hanging in his bedroom, which he meditates on when he dreams about being out of the hospital.

Glenn also enjoys going to the movies. Together, we have seen *Stop Or My Mom Will Shoot, A League of Their Own, Sister Act, Wayne's World* and *Beethoven.* He has seen all the *Star Trek* movies more than once. He likes science fiction movies the most, and dramatic movies the least.

His favorite sport is probably baseball, and being from Baltimore, he is a diehard Baltimore Oriole fan. If he were able to choose a position on a baseball team, he would play center field, "because that's what I'm used to playing. And I don't want to be a pitcher, cause in the major leagues when you pitch, then you can't bat." His favorite basketball team without any question is the Chicago Bulls, and among the college teams, the Duke University Blue Devils. The team he likes to watch play hockey in the NHL (National Hockey League) is the Baltimore Skipjacks.

If he had a pet, he would like to have a monkey. In his home, he remembers having had a dog, cat, and birds. But he would like a monkey: "My aunt had one, my mother's aunt had one. And my mother's friend had one. That's what I want: I want to go to the zoo."

Glenn is concerned not only with his own life, but also with the environment, and what we are doing to the world, and therefore to ourselves: "If you stop'em at the bottom, like with the sun. Then everything'll die. All the animals'll die, and then we'll die. Ain't the earth supposed to end by burnin' up? That's what I've heard." I answered that I was not sure when the world was going to burn up, or how it will burn up. I then asked him if he thought God wants to see the earth end, and if not, why not:

> Because He loves us and he don't want to see all of us die. And he made this earth for us. See, what I don't understand . . . He made the earth for us, why can't he just throw in an extra layer of the ozone?

I said that we had been given one chance with one ozone: "Do you think if we got another chance, we would learn from it?" Glenn answered in a depressing tone of voice: "No."

However, as I began to know Glenn, or as Glenn started to reveal more of himself underneath a surface impression, I learned what he would like to do most in the world, the answer would be "Return home!" He misses living in Baltimore, and talks often about the house he was raised in with his five brothers, his mother, and for a short period of time his grandmother. Unfortunately, it was at home that Glenn first learned to use drugs, like marijuana, along with other members of the family. By the time that Glenn was nine years-old, he, along with his brothers and his mother, was addicted to a life of various drugs.

His addiction to drugs has continued to follow him into institutional life. For example, one Saturday, there was a surprise "inspection" of his room by the hospital staff, and an empty sandwich bag that did have drugs in it was found under his bed mattress. Glenn "swore" that he did not take any drugs, and they were already in his room when he moved into it two months ago. He knows that he should be careful about what he does and who his friends are, and where he lives: "Say I've rented a room at a motel, and the people who used to be in there had drugs and they hid it, and they came in and they found the drugs . . . I could have got locked up for it." After they did a urine test on Glenn, finding nothing in his system, they told Glenn that he was innocent.

I asked him if he felt anyone condemn him for what he had done? "One staff. He ain't sayin' that but he just doesn't talk to me." I asked Glenn if it hurt him at all: "Yeah, a little bit." What Glenn needs is a drug rehab program, but there is none available at the institution. Will Glenn go back to doing drugs once he leaves the hospital? "I don't know. It depends on the situation." I asked him if it was hard not to go back onto drugs: "Yeah." It is hard, because Glenn is addicted to drugs.

Like other young people in his generation, Glenn grew up on heavy metal music, and bands like Metallica, Ozzie Osborne, and Motley Crue. It was during our discussion over what music he liked and did not like that his understanding of God, Satan, Jesus, good and evil began to emerge. In one session, Glenn explained—or deciphered and translated—for me the meaning behind the symbols on CD covers, keychains, and T-shirts:

> [The pentagram] is supposed to be the sign of worshipping the devil. I don't have no pentagrams, or upside down crosses . . . [all I have] is just a sword with a snake on it. And the snake has a monster on its head. The face of it is like a monster.

When I asked Glenn what he liked about it, he said "I grew up on it . . . I used to listen to Ozzie Osborne too, but then I . . . realized that the upside down crosses were on his albums and all . . . I don't listen to him no more. "

Glenn explained that the reason people worship the devil is because "some people do it because other people's doin' it, and they think the other peoples doin' it. Or say, someone has prayed and prayed and prayed, and nuttin' ever happened, so they don't think there is a God, so they turn to worship the devil."

In the midst of this ordinary, personal narrative of a young adolescent who grew up listening and taking in a daily dose of loud, heavy metal music, partaking in the revolving door of drugs in his home, and growing up in the lower socio-economic, inner-city area of Baltimore in a home where the mother had hooked her son on drugs and the father was absent, with no drive, no incentive for bettering one's life, the stunningly miraculous aspect of Glenn's life is that he believes in God. It suddenly dawned upon me in our conversations that drugs were not the only thing that started at home. It is also in his home that his Christian journey began. Somehow or other Glenn was baptized when he was a child, or so his mother told him. "I was too young to know what was going on," he said. He was envious of those who were baptized in a pool of water, wanting to know if pastors ever just let people stay under the water to scare them.

Fragmented ideas and images about God and Jesus continued to be added and shaped when he was placed in a halfway home of sorts for children with emotional disabilities before he came to his current placement. He lived in a manor house that was part of a monastery, and he and his friends used to run around the church, playing hide-and-go-seek among the confessional booths and the pews in the darkened sanctuary . . . as well as spooking one another.

When I asked Glenn to draw a picture of God, he kept on apologizing, saying "I'm not too good at drawing this stuff." He sometimes confused God, Jesus, and the Holy Spirit in trying to capture one of the three in his design. He remembered seeing pictures in the stained-glass windows of churches of a "white bird" and of a man with a beard, holding a sheep. His picture of Jesus had a halo on his head, and a crown, "because they keep on calling him a king. He's mightier than I am. [And] everyone looks up to him, I guess. Everyone in heaven looks up to him. I can't draw it." As he drew the picture, Glenn said that he thought God was alive at Devereux, though he was not sure when was the last time he saw him. God, to Glenn, is an older man, with a heart, and "is only scary to think about in funerals."

Had he ever seen God? Glenn said that once, right before she died, his grandmother claimed to have seen God: "We kind of laughed at her about it, but she was real serious. My grandma lived downstairs in a hospital bed in our house. She died right after she told us what she had seen."

Did God have anything to do with the creation of the world? Glenn smiled, nonchalantly saying "Yeah, I think so. I think the creation of the world happened like . . . when I saw the movie *Fantasia* . . . I think it was just like that." With that, he drew a picture of a large dinosaur, looking more like a brontosaurus than anything else, stalking the earth. As he stared at the picture he had just drawn, Glenn talks about the order of the creation of nature:

> I believe God is alive now. I believe He's here, but He's kinda dead. Not alive. I don't know because people say, like back, then, the people that hung him on a cross, they had to be some sort of people. And then people must have died out, and then came the dinosaurs . . . or something [like that].

I said that it was probably dinosaurs first, and then people. Glenn was intrigued with the question of creation: "Who made the dinosaurs?" he asked. "Well, God did," I said. "But how, if God was still a person?" Glenn asked. And the questions of the nature of God continue to arise in our discussions.

The evidence for God's existence in our world that Glenn needed to truly believe in the presence of God came through the most unlikely yet natural source for Glenn: through the music of Motley Crue:

> There's this one song, called "Shout at the Devil." I mean, it's not worshipping him, but it's . . . at the beginning it says something like . . . I remember it saying "and return with revenge to shout at the devil." And they cuss a lot, [but] not at God.

Glenn is intrigued at not only the ways God can be known, but that God is known in so many different parts of the world, in different ways, and throughout time. For example, one session Glenn told me that God probably plays a whole bunch of sports, "not just basketball." From being the questioner, Glenn turned the tables and started to ask me questions about God. "Is there like people from different countries who believe in different things? Like people in China, do they believe in God? Or do people in Greece, do they believe in our God, or just Zeus like in the myths?"

During our final conversations together, Glenn revealed that he still has dreams of helping not only himself, but others as well. For example, what does Glenn want to be when he grows up? He wants to be a lawyer. What kind? "A lawyer, you know, helping kids . . . kids like us, like being a drug counselor," he says.

On our last time out together from the hospital, before Glenn had to leave to move to another program which was far less restrictive than the one he was in, we went out to see the Whoopi Goldberg movie *Sister Act*, and then to McDonald's for lunch, where he thanked me for being his friend at the hospital. When I asked him what he was going to miss in leaving this place, he smiled and said "Everyone."

• • •

My time with Glenn revealed the unpredictable nature of life. Who could have predicted that in a home where drugs became the mainstay of family life, that signs and effects of God's presence would be discovered? It is as if Glenn discovered God by mistake, bumping into God while running around, playing hide-and-go-seek in a darkened sanctuary attached to a manor house for young children with emotional disabilities. Since that time God has been following Glenn from home, to manor house, to a hospital, to a halfway house, and beyond.

Something wonderful probably happened in such moments in the games Glenn played with his friend in a small Catholic church outside Baltimore. For even the simple pictures of a dove in a stained-glass window, or a song about the "King of Kings" made a deeper imprint upon his soul than anyone could have thought of—or planned for. In such games we not only play with God, but God also comes and plays with us, a game where God is revealed, and our lives are never the same, again.

10

Turning Cheeks

But if anyone strikes you on the right cheek, turn the other also (Matt. 5:38).

Recently, I got punched in the face by a disabled child. Stephanie had had her fill of a group therapy session, especially in her fractious relationship with another young woman. The fist that hit my face was not intended for me at all. I was in the middle of a vicious shouting match, getting one young girl to sit down and cool her heels, while her sparring partner was being cooled down by her friends. Suddenly, an unexpected head came out of the left side of the room, and a young boy who wanted to see the fight continue and build in its fury charged me from the left side, knocking me surprised and breathless to the ground, allowing the two young women to begin hitting one another again.

Standing up, I was then hit in the face with my glasses on, not once but twice, and soon I was lost in the chaotic tussle of young people trying to stop the fight. In the next minute, as I held my face, I soon found that I was part of a flow of youngsters pushing the one girl down on the floor. In one swift motion, the staff forcefully pinned down the other girl to the floor. Once the room was vacated, I picked up my glasses only to find them all bent out of shape, looking like a Picassoesque vision of wire-framed, horn-rimmed glasses. My forehead had a bright red mark where the punch landed. I was anxious and a bit frayed around the edges. A most violent way to begin a Monday morning.

Following the fight, I went to debrief with the rest of the staff involved in the confrontation. Even though I have had the required classes on crisis prevention and intervention, and learned all the "therapeutic holding" moves used for controlling physical confrontations, I chose not to use the techniques, because of the subtle physical, violent aggression hidden under the rubric of "safety."[1] The staff unanimously declared that I had done nothing, which they thought was foolish on my part. My response was that I *did* do something: I talked to the young women and refused to be threatened or intimidated by their verbal threats to me and one another. I responded with nonviolence, and this can make all the difference in the world. Why not put the words of Jesus into practice? I simply turned the other cheek to the ugly, raging violence of the group. No one was satisfied with the answer.

Things did not calm down that much for Stephanie during the day. When I checked in with her toward evening, I asked if she had some time to talk with me. We went to a quiet room on the unit. When I closed the door to the room, she let forth with a fiery verbal assault, exposing how lonely and vulnerable she felt, stressing that there was no support for her in her isolation and loneliness. Known for exaggerating situations, Stephanie spewed forth her anger, spitting out her words like a blast of singeing fire. I said nothing, alternately looking at her and glancing to the floor, hoping that she would get it out of her system. "You don't care for me when you leave this place. God doesn't care for me or He would have rescued me by now from this hellish place; Jesus doesn't care about me either. *No* one cares about me in this place," she said angrily. This was followed by a great burst of tears and uncontrollable sobbing, to be softened by the only equipment I had: a box of tissues. Sitting calmly, struggling to be with her in her hurt and not saying a word, was enough to vanquish the dragon within Stephanie. We were reconciled.

Recently, Stephanie left the hospital for a new placement. I had a chance to ask her what she had learned from this wrenching episode:

> Most people who say "I'm a brother of God," or "I'm a sister of God's," or "I'm a man of God," if something like that happened to them, they would have held a grudge . . . acting real nasty and cruel. I'm really sorry I broke your glasses; I'm real sorry about that. Even though that happened, you knew what was going on with me, and you didn't [leave me]. I want to thank you for that, for being a true friend.

Working with young people who have what society has labeled "be-havioral disorders" has, in many secular, institutional settings, become a more violent game, where the cry of the day is "Safety first!" rather than the more compassionate, professional refrain: "First, do no harm." It is violent because the young people who come to many of the residen-tial treatment centers for behavior disorders are more violent in both their verbal and physical gestures. The violent edge among these youngsters comes from the homes and communities that have nurtured and shaped their very character, where "education" includes a "how-to" manual in survival, with physical and verbal aggression at the top of the list. These young people understand the world as the eternally competitive game of "survival of the fittest." Fists, guns, and knives are all effective in playing this game of life.

Life in our institutions for people with disabilities is often a micro-cosmic reflection of the searing rage surrounding the walls of our bu-colic group homes and sheltered institutions. Like life on the city streets, there are two players in many centers for children and adoles-cents with behavioral disorders: the staff meets the violence of the street kids with equal violence and raging force. The problem in an-swering the young people with such violence or force is that violence begets violence. Violence does not deter more violence; it just makes people think of more ways to be violent against the "other."

Our character is shaped by the violent society that forms us. This is why Jesus' call to turn the other cheek is such a radical departure. Jesus addressed our human impulse to retaliate against violence, with its eye-for-an-eye philosophy, telling his followers that if *anyone* strikes you on the right cheek, turn the other also (Luke 6:29; Matthew 5:38). Instead, we are to love our enemies as well as those who persecute us and watch for our failings to emerge. This "anyone" includes *even* children and adolescents, whatever their disorders or limitations.

The theologian Stanley Hauerwas has said that we turn the other cheek not because it feels good, but because it is the right thing to do—because this is the way of God in Christ: "Cheek turning is not advocated as what works (it usually does not), but advocated because this is the way God is—God is kind to the ungrateful and the selfish." It is one thing to *read* these words and say "I can do that." It is a wholly other thing to follow through in *acting* on these words of Jesus in the midst of violence. Yet it is the essential gesture of turning the cheek that exposes us for who we are: members of the community of Christ; alien residents, indeed.

In acting on these words of Jesus, turning the other cheek and getting hit in the face, I confounded the common wisdom of the people on the unit, staff and children alike, who expected me to force the child down on the ground rather than get hit in the face. But can we not act from love rather than fear? Not hitting or forcefully pushing the child into a prone position, not pinning her down until she was placed in four-point restraints, invites the more radical step of not hitting or lashing out at *anyone*.

The violence and anger we meet on the units of a hospital for children and adolescents with behavioral problems are the same urgent forces that enflame and confront our racially divided country, as was observed in the riots following the original Rodney King verdict in parts of Los Angeles. My hospital is merely a microcosmic reflection of a strife-torn society that, rather than celebrating diversity, fears those who are different from "you and me" as deviant and grotesque.

"Turning the cheek" is easy to read about. Yet it goes against everything in us that encourages us to lash out and to hit back, to control and sequester the anger of the dragon in the other person. But to be vulnerable, to receive the pain of another as it shoots forth in unbridled rage, to lay down one's life for another person, is the ultimate gift of love.

As Christians, in all our various vocations, to live our lives according to God's vision of the world is an incredible struggle that seems to never end: to do good to those who hate us, to bless those who curse and abuse us; to give what we have when people beg; "to do to others as you would have them do to you" (Luke 6:27–31). These words are treasonous in the eyes of many. Living these words will cause people on the streets to point and stare at us, to dismiss us as crazy for following such a logic. We *are* a danger to the law and order of the world that we find ourselves in. Some of us, at any rate, could well lose our jobs if we do not "smarten up!" And Jesus? He instructs us, come what may, to live a merciful life "just as your Father is merciful" (Luke 6:36). So let us continue to do the unthinkable, speak the unmentionable, and live the unreasonable—according to the world. For we are members, one with another, of a gathering of Christian cheek-turners.

11

And Jesus Said, "Come to Me"

Come to me, all you that are weary and are carrying heavy burdens, and I will give you rest. Take my yoke upon you, and learn from me; for I am gentle and humble in heart, and you will find rest for your souls. For my yoke is easy, and my burden is light (Matthew 11:28–30, NRSV).

As has been written and hinted at in other parts of this book, one of the continuing themes that has surfaced in talking with and listening to young adolescents with behavioral and emotional disorders is the search for a resting place in their lives. These children strike me as those who could be described as the "neediest of the needy," for their most basic need is not being fulfilled: of a caring, nurturing, supportive, healthy, loving community that they could call home. My experience of these young people is that they are exhausted by and tired of the journey. They have been taken away from their biological mother and father, as well as their natural family, for various reasons and causes: from abuse in the family, to poor economic conditions. They have only begun to trek through the often arid, barren land of health service providers. Some have been to a multitude of therapeutic foster homes, in which either the child did not fit the family, or the family did not fit the child, and there was abuse or the child simply ran away from the situation to the streets. Others, having exhausted the foster home alternative, have been to various institutions and group homes. However, institutionalized health care in other settings did not seem to quiet the soul of the child. And so this setting is either another place on their trek toward a variety of other situations, or sometimes the child is lucky and it is the place that helps them enough to get home. Until they find this home, this resting place on the journey, these children will act out and react in a scattered, schizophrenic-like, violent outburst that hurts and abuses others. And there is no remorse in their eyes: for they are hurt, terrified of the loss of place called "home."

Before they can find this haven, this sanctuary, they wait to hear an invitation from someone, somewhere to them. Without the invitation, a reaching out, they do not know where they can go or turn for help. In some ways, they are like a person thrown out of a boat into the middle of the ocean, and after some time in the water they are close to drowning as the waters swirl around them and waves crash in a drenching cycle. In response to this terrifying sensation of drowning, they begin to thrash mightily and clumsily in the water, scared of what is their fate. There is the look of sheer terror in their eyes and their actions as they feel themselves slipping from consciousness. It is this violent thrashing about that staff and other children get caught in when they try to reach out and extend arms of love to the drowning person.

Many Christians know this sense of abandonment in the open seas of life. They know the terror of loneliness, and are well-practiced in the physical and emotional act of thrashing. That is why the words of Jesus, "Come to me," unleashes the hopes and fears of people. Tears rolling down our cheeks, we hear and read Jesus say "Come to me" again and again, not believing that we have heard it correctly the first time. Surprised by the holy invitation, we begin to laugh and cry at the same time, for we have discovered that we are Christ's own.

One who has been caught off guard yet is thrilled at hearing these words, with the dawning realization that it is extended to her, is Stephanie, the young African-American woman whose poetry happily taunts the presuppositions of Christian leaders (see "Pilgrims Lost in an Alien Land"). Stephanie's life has been filled with much pain: she had an abortion in her early teenage years; she has said that she has been sexually abused; and she and her mother are in a constant, tense state of antagonism. On top of it all, Stephanie has lived in various places, attended many schools suited for such young people with emotional problems. Because of her background, Stephanie is a young woman who tries to be all things to all people some days of the week, and is stubbornly herself other days of the week, with little indication of which mood she is in when one talks with her. She is one who is well known for thrashing about on the hospital unit, verbally as well as physically abusing other young people out of her fear and loneliness. Yet in the chaotic waters of life that she feels embedded in, there is the slightest recognition of faith that God in Christ is calling to her and saying "Come to me."

Evidence of this weak yet still-present faith is supported in our many conversations, which occurred on days that Stephanie felt she was, in her own words, "walking with the Lord," and days where all of us were her enemies and she had no friends on the face of the earth. What drew my attention to Stephanie and her story of faith is Stephanie's skill as a creative personality. She is a dancer who takes tap, ballet, and jazz lessons on the unit, which is a therapeutic release for her of sorts. She also writes and reads poetry, with Maya Angelou as a model poet. She confessed early on in our relationship that "God knows what I'm capable of, and He knows my vivid imagination."

Stephanie knew that to get my attention all she had to say was that she wanted to talk about God, or did not believe any more in God. Since our first sit-down conversation, I have come to see that Stephanie has many engagingly creative thoughts about the nature of God, God's relationship to Jesus and the Holy Spirit, as well as love, friendship, and other assorted characteristics of life:

> God, over all, is our Maker, and He's my savior. Um, God's a spirit. He's everywhere. You can't get rid of Him. You can't ask Him to leave, because He won't. It's just a matter of you saying that you want Him in your life and that you're willing to go by His rules. I think He's a selfish God, though . . . because . . . I was reading in the Bible, how you know, He does not want you to love anyone greater than you love Him. And true, He does a lot, true He keeps me out of trouble, true He holds my hand when I have no one else's hand to hold . . . God has shown me how much trouble I can get into without Him. When I've strayed away from Him, and decided to go about my simple little way, I feel bad, I get into trouble, I get into fights, things will be blamed on me that I didn't even do. Then once I say wait a minute, I forgot to pray, I forgot to say thanks for this, I forgot to say thank you Lord for making sure that I got to and from school safely today. Then once I do that, and I say, Lord, I know I haven't talked to you in a while, but I'm talking to you now, and I'm sorry, and I do love you, then things just seem to smoothen' out. Some people think that's just a little mind game that you play with yourself, that you

think that maybe after you talk to God that things smooth out.
But no, it's not. God is real!

What does Stephanie think about Jesus?

> I see Jesus as a flunky for God. For Jesus is God's son. I see him as
> when, I feel like I can't talk to God, which is the BIG man, and
> I feel that maybe I need to talk to someone that's maybe a little
> more understanding than maybe God is, a little more forgiving,
> because God expects so much out of you. Then I can talk to Jesus.

As for the Holy Spirit, "that's just a feeling that you get. You can't
put it into words, that's feelings . . . of security."

When asked if Stephanie had ever experienced God, she says that
God is there when she looks like she is upset and she's crying because
she is so happy "because God has just touched me, and you know, I
know that He has and I'm happy that he decided to touch me."

Though she feels lonely on the unit, unable to talk to many of the
other young people about God, because they do not believe "like I
do," she has found the most support for her faith in the church, "where
you have altar calls and stuff like that. And you go up, and . . . because
in my church . . . you all go up and everyone will get on their knees
around the altar, and then you're to call out the person's name that
you're praying for."

While Stephanie wants to be close to God some days, there are
other moments when she feels free to wander. Her mother has told her
that "once I get closer to God, and once He's closer to me, and He
knows that I'm gonna stay for a while," then life will be better for her.
Yet she admits to her wanderlust spirit:

> I stray away so much that maybe He'll teach me how to understand
> his word better. My mother gave me this prayer to say before I read
> my scriptures: Lord help me to understand your Word, in thy Name
> I pray. Amen.

There is this tension, of not being faithful to God, "doing things that
I know are against His will." Then, she turns around in the next
sentence and says that she "strongly believes in God. I read his word
because I believe that He is real, and I believe that his love and mercy
for us is real. Because if it's not, then I would have been dead by now."

Her favorite Psalm for the day echoes her sentiment: "If it had not been the Lord who was on our side, when our enemies attacked us, then they would have swallowed us up alive" (Psalm 124:2,3).

Faith and Forgiveness

After a surprising conversation around deeply meaningful theological insights into the nature of God, and human freedom to express faith in God one day, another day brought forth the frustrating moments with Stephanie as she revealed her contempt for God in another conversation. Stephanie had heard that she might be moved to a facility closer to home, but the decision is being made by her mother and the social worker, not by her, and she is angry about her inability to voice her opinion: she feels shut out of the deciding loop.

In response to the question, if she wanted to talk about God, Stephanie said "Let's talk about why I think God has said, 'Fuck me.'" After I told her that I never heard God swear before, she said "Let's talk about why I think He's left me alone . . . and how lonely I feel because He's left me, and how much trouble I'm getting into because of that and all those sins I'm committing. Is having sex before you get married a sin?"

I backed up to talk about what is sin to Stephanie: "Things that are not in God's Ten Commandments and will," she said. Yet to Stephanie, sexual intercourse with the one she loved is not a sin: "People have hormones, people have urges, people . . . I mean if God made people He should have known that . . . everybody wasn't going to be perfect."

When I talked about forgiveness, that did not stop the questions: "Don't you ever think that you may do something one time that is . . . unforgivable?" I asked her to clarify what she was saying, but that did not help her: "I don't know. I'm confused." Trying to backtrack, I asked her if people were either born good or bad: "Good and bad," she said. Behind all these pointed questions about God's love and human sin is Stephanie's history of having had an abortion, which is still on her mind and heart, and she has not quite forgiven herself for it. She realizes that, at the age of sixteen, the baby would have been three years-old: "Only by the mercy of God, I'm still here," she said.

· · ·

For the next two times we met, she drew pictures of creation, God, and Jesus. In these colorful and symbolic pictures, one continues to get a better glimpse of her creative ability as well as insight into her theological worldview.

In her drawing of creation, everything was clean and orderly. Her creation was pretty. After drawing her image of creation, she told me her version of the creation story, or more accurately a cosmological worldview:

> In the beginning God created the trees, and the grass, and the sand, and restored all the water and stuff in the seas and in the ocean, and made it clean. Then next, he restored the animals, the birds and stuff, and all the birds or animals, like sea cows and stuff that get hurt . . . (like the manatees) he fixes them and stuff. Then he creates the first man, and the man would teach other animals how not to hurt each other and stuff. Then he create a woman, and she take care of all the flowers and stuff, she be like . . . the master gardener. And she can fix plants and stuff. The man was black and the woman was Indian. And then, then they'd have children, and then good children taught . . . the children grew up and then they had children and then they taught their children, and then their children had children until we had a whole big population. (How did sin come in to this world?) One of the children hurt somebody else . . . willingly. Through hatred and jealousy, and then that's how they discovered that feeling of hating, or wanting to hurt someone or wanting to kill someone or something. [The punishment is] they will be thrown into hell. You get three chances [to improve yourself], and three strikes and your out.

Explaining her picture of God, Stephanie described it as such:

> God has a beard, I mean a tremendously long beard. And I think it's a beard of all the sins of the people, and I think he sticks them [the sins] in here. That's what makes his beard so long. He has a long beard, and long hair, and no nose [but has eyes].

I asked her if God has ears: "Of course he has ears, or he couldn't hear our prayers! And he has this light that goes everywhere, like an aura . . . or a shaft of light." Her image of God has no body "because we're God's hands and feet." The picture of Jesus had a body and hair of branches like a tree:

See, Jesus, instead of God with the long beard, Jesus has this head piece, and I'm all a piece of his head . . . this big crown he wears. And when I start to sin, the branches start to grow, and the more I sin, and then he reaches out to the branches. And when I ask for forgiveness, and he knows that I'm sorry, that I would like him to forgive me, he takes it back. Sometimes, his crown is real full because people forget to say I'm sorry. But then sometimes, it come close to the root.

It was during this conversation that we got to talking about Jesus' relationship with Stephanie: Jesus makes Stephanie sing, "because singing makes me happy, and Jesus wants to make me happy." I asked her how she makes Jesus happy? "By obeying God's word." And then I asked her what word it was, and she quoted the verse from Matthew 11: "Come unto me. Good words to hear, when I think he's there," she said. She admitted to feeling abandoned, left alone by Jesus some times. She yearns to hear the words, "Come unto me." And that is where she places her life, in the place of great tension, between giving all and coming unto Jesus and resting in him, and trying to do it all on her own, which leaves her feeling abandoned.

In our last time together, before she was discharged to live closer to home, Stephanie's talk was of a stronger faith, promising me that one of her goals "is to go to church once a week, so that I can just thank the Lord in his house, thank him for all of my large blessings, and thank him for my health and for my talents, and ask him to hold my hand, cause I'm going to need a lot of it."

●　●　●

As Stephanie left the hospital, it was doubtful that she would keep her word of going to church. This is not because she would not want to attend congregational worship. It is because she is unable to attend and find the strength or will to reach out and accept Jesus' kind invitation to come to him. Stephanie's faith is like any other Christian's faith: the act of responding to Jesus' call to "Come to me," and live in him is not meant to be an individualistic, extracurricular activity. It is a profound act of Jesus Christ's caring community; it is the act of Christ's community, a community of people who know God's gift of grace, and therefore can gather around each other in order to truly and lovingly support one another in response to "Come to me."

Why is acknowledging Christ's call to come to him, an act of the Christian community? Because we need the supportive faith of others in Christ to carry us through with this most unnatural action. The community of Christ who believes in God can alone help us in our hours of disbelief, for they have been there too. The community of Christ reminds us to love each other as Christ first loved us.

12

The Religious Narratives of Disabled Adolescents

What has been the religious experience of adolescents who have been labeled as having "behavioral disorders"? In many therapeutic settings, a young person's response to this question about their ideas and impressions regarding their experiences of God or other religious phenomena has been interpreted in a myriad of ways, depending on the worldview of the therapist or psychiatrist. Some health care professionals like social workers, special educators, psychologists, and psychiatrists first consider that the young person has a disabling condition, and then listen to the response with this bias in place. Most responses are perceived as symptomatic or a result of the child's disabling conditions.

For example, the psychiatrist William Meissner suggests that belief systems are a natural part of the human condition. However, he also believes that there is a point in the life of some people where the belief system can easily become a powerful vehicle used by the unconscious to prevent or subvert effective, adaptive functioning. Where exactly that point is, Meissner does not tell the reader. What Meissner is trying to determine is the extent of an adolescent's neurosis, and then analyze components of the adolescent's religious narrative in describing neurotic religious involvement.[1]

Sigmund Freud argued that religion is a neurosis based on wishes . . . feelings of both submission and dependence.[2] Freud suggested that religion as a whole is an intellectual delusion, "fulfillments of the oldest, strongest, and most urgent wishes of mankind."[3] Other psychiatrists like Ana-Maria Rizzuto look at God and religion as illusions each person selects to reveal his or her personal history; religion and God are the "resting place" in which one lives and has his or her being. The private God of each person has the potential to provide "silent communication, thus increasing our sense of being real."[4]

Even the child psychologist Jean Piaget wrote that children attribute to their parents the perfections and attributes which they will later transfer to God.[5]

The tendency in the Freudian and Piagetian paradigm is to let either the disabling condition of a person or the age of the child prejudge the authenticity of one's perception of reality, let alone religious experiences.

Even though a person may have a disability of mind and body, like a behavior disorder that is treatable by psychological, educational, or medical intervention, does it mean that one's faith is a vehicle for a powerful unconscious fantasy, or is an intellectual delusion of a primary infantile sentiment? Many professionals using the medical model in general, and the psychiatric model in particular, perceive faith as primarily a cognitive or affective function of the mind; a human trait that can be controlled by our unconsciousness. With this perception, it is assumed that if one's affect or cognition is disabled, then one's ideas about God may certainly be compromised. One's faith in God may be judged to be unstable if it is reduced to figments of imagination or a construction of an individual's mind.

The assumption that faith is solely a cognitive or affective function has been questioned by many theologians and professionals in health care. Theologians argue that faith is not solely a construct of the mind, something that develops in a Piagetian linear, stagelike sequence of development. Faith is understood as God's gift to humankind. Among professionals in the health care field, some are even suggesting that spiritual awareness, or more precisely an awareness of God, is only marginally related to intelligence, if at all.[6] Instead, faith, while influencing those aspects of our nature attributed to our bodies and minds, is not totally dependent upon human intelligence. Faith is much more than a construct of the human imagination. Faith is a gift to humankind, which is corporate in nature as it is shaped and nurtured in a religious community.

The question regarding the religious experiences of young people with behavioral disorders is raised anew because, in working with these young people with this disability in an institutional setting, their responses to questions about God and Jesus, life and death, are not necessarily psychopathological or "troubled" in nature. Instead, conversations with them about God and life are often insightful, reasonable, logical, and systematic. What is even more surprising is the indomitable nature of these children's faith in God even in a surrounding culture that emphasizes the neutrality of all values within a strongly controlled medical-behavioral model of care. The young people in this controlled, value-neutral culture have been asking God certain questions about life even *without* the benefit of the company of a religious community.

For example, in one of the preceding chapters, "A Poet among Us," there is the story of Ben: Young Ben is white and Jewish. We began our relationship when he discovered my interest in religion and stories. A poet at heart, he would come into my office and sat in my rocking chair, rocking wildly to and fro. Often we read some poetry by Robert Frost, and he started to slow down in his rocking. He then asked if he could write a poem for me, à la Robert Frost, with somber thoughts of life and death:

> The day awaits the churning tide,
> The day awaits the moon's arise,
> The sun awaits the moon's desist,
> Rising through the midnight mist.
>
> The earth awaits the warmth and light,
> Rising through the mist of night.
> And as the game comes to a close,
> The world plays the game still nobody knows.
> As my black heart beats the juices I yearn,
> As something in me begins to turn.
>
> A child is born unlike the rest,
> The someone who threatens the beat in my chest,
> Am I destined to die or destined to find,
> the mortal who dares to open the human mind?

Or consider Kenzie's story: Kenzie is a fifteen year old Baptist. I am sitting, listening to a discussion on TV shows in a community therapeutic meeting. There is a break in the meeting, and Kenzie gets up. She has been advocating for the right of the adolescents on the unit to watch "Married . . . with Children" on Sunday night, with little movement in the opinion of the staff. She gets up from her chair in the meeting square, and goes over to her room, gets her white Bible, and comes back, thrusting the Bible toward me, saying "Find me a verse from the Bible to calm myself down. I'm just mad and need something to put this in perspective. Find something quick." It was as if I were a medical doctor trying to unwrap the syringe to quickly give her a shot to calm down. I found the medicine I needed in the book of Psalms. I hit upon Psalm 23, "thy rod and thy staff they comfort me," I read. She is sort of satisfied, but not enough; she wants more. She tells me to look up the part in the Bible where Jesus talks about "not being anxious . . . taking burdens . . . read that part." So I read this passage in which Jesus says to "take my yoke upon you, and I will give you rest" (Matt. 11:28). She tells me this is the verse her mother read to her when she was a child; it used to make Kenzie feel good about herself. Calmed down enough, the meeting resumes, and Kenzie, again, advocates for her friends in the meeting.

This chapter is on the religious narrative of adolescents with one of the disabilities under the broad umbrella of behavioral disorders living in an institutional setting. The power of these narratives is found in the insightful, logical, reasoning of young people who have been placed in the context of a hospital for those judged to be too "disturbed" to function "normally" in another context. What these narratives reveal are several engaging and enlightening portrayals of young people's faith, first nurtured in the midst of their home congregation or parish, that have survived even the isolation of life behind the walls of an institution.

In the following section there will be a brief description of conversations that the researcher has had with the young people, along with a formal interview.[7] In the second section, there will be a discussion of some of the common characteristics of these religious narratives as they are perceived in the lives of these young people while living in an institution. In sum, these brief stories show us the convincing power of the young people's faith through their ongoing religious narrative.

An Initial Reading of Religious Narratives

In the field of theological studies, the term "religious" or "spiritual" narrative has been quite widely used lately. The child psychiatrist Robert Coles describes the "spiritual life" as the capacity to be aware of the presence of the Holy.[8] The educator John Dewey used the term "religious" as an adjective, versus the noun "religion," which signifies a special body of beliefs and practices having some kind of institutional organization.[9] "Religious" points to an experience of something or someone, like God, Jesus, or Buddha, in the context of a community of faith, not as something that exists freely by itself.

According to the theologian Stanley Hauerwas, "narrative" is more than merely telling a story. A narrative is a mode of moral reflection; a crucial concept for revealing aspects of a person's character.[10] The theologian Garrett Green suggests that our human narratives function paradigmatically, revealing the essential pattern of a person's life.[11] In this chapter about a child's or adolescent's religious narrative, the focus is on both the context and content of the religious nature of the narrative, in this case a child's experience of God in the context of a church or synagogue, revealed in the very telling of the story. By listening to the child's story, the reader may learn something about the meaningful pattern of a child's life.

The religious narratives that will be shared are beginnings of longer conversations. The method of collecting these narratives is by the "wait, watch, and listen" method. While I let the children and adolescents know what it is that I am trying to learn, which is primarily their religious story, I approach this task by waiting to meet them, attending community meetings, visiting the units late at night and on Sundays again, *being with them* rather than trying to do something *to and for them.*

The following religious narratives are by young people who have these things in common: first, they have all been diagnosed and labeled as having behavioral disorders due to either physiological manifestations or abusive home situations. Second, these children are all experiencing what could be called an "interruption" in life, taken out of their families and communities, and placed in the artificial context of an institution. Third, these are all young people, between the ages of five to eighteen years old, who are living away not only from their family and friends, but also from church and synagogue.

Ben

Reconsider Ben, who is Jewish and referred to earlier in the book. He has participated in the Bar Mitzvah ritual in the Reformed Jewish temple his family attends. In the eyes of this community and God, Ben is a man.

As has also been made known in the previous chapters, Ben is a poet, understanding and interpreting the world through the rhythm of the words of a poet. But as a poet, he is also a person who easily gets frustrated with which words to use and when to use them.

When asking him about his memories of growing up in temple, the one thing that he liked was all the reading during worship. The biggest lesson that he learned in attending his parents synagogue was how to speak Hebrew, for it is through the words of the Torah that he "knows God."

When asked about his impression of God one day, Ben experiences God as spirit and mystery, "because God works in mysterious ways. For example, take my grandpa; when he was dying, we prayed for him to be healed, and he was made well. How can you explain that? Or take creation . . . it's all mystery."

Dale

Dale found me; I did not find Dale. In a funny way, I was the answer to Dale's dreams, for he is a terribly religious person who truly believes that religion, magic in particular, is what is going to finally make him well.

Like Ben, Dale is Jewish, with his "Jewishness" being rather conditional in nature. Currently, he describes himself as "Jewish Buddhist, with an interest in Ninja (a martial art)." At the hospital, Dale has a reputation for believing in anything that grants him magical power, whether it is white magic or black magic. But lately in our conversations he has turned to world religions, first Buddhism, and now back to his roots of Judaism. Why Judaism? "Because the Jews are God's chosen people. I'm one of the chosen by God. That's why I'm in it."

When asked to describe God, Dale, like Ben, envisioned God as spirit, telling me, "You can't see spirit." Earlier in the week, when shown a picture of Michelangelo's "God" from the *Life* story on the Sistine Chapel (November 1991), I asked Dale if *this* was what God looked like to him. Dale was quick to respond, looking straight in my eyes: "No. That's not God. God's spirit, not a person. He's almighty." When I asked Dale to tell me how he experiences God if God's a spirit, he said, "I feel good in myself . . . my whole soul feels good."

Kenzie

After the first week at the institution, Kenzie decided that she could talk to me about God, "since no one else can talk about God."

Kenzie grew up in an African-American congregation. What she likes about going to church is that she is always "learning something that I need to know about God. We learn about the future from God, and what will happen to those who do and don't believe in God."

Her favorite activity in going to church is singing in the choir, though "us young kids aren't allowed in the choir? I don't think that's fair, you know what I mean?" Her favorite songs, which she sang, are "Soon, oh very soon, we are going to see the King." She likes to sing fast in church, and shout "Praise the Lord" in church: "Some people can fake faith, by just shouting. But there's this one woman who always gets us going. She ain't fakin' it, either." She tried "Catholic" but thought it was boring compared to the singing and shouting in her church.

Kenzie is aware of God always being with her:

> God is not a person but a presence; a voice; One who is watching over me, and can see the future and the past. God is like a conscience, like these little angels on the shoulder, the one on the right is the good angel, telling you what you should do; the one on the left telling you to do something bad. My mama told me to listen to the one on the right. And there is nothing that He misses. God is like a big voice with hands. He causes us to do things that aren't right [in order for us] to learn. I believe in the devil, too, but not in what he's doing on earth.

What Kenzie likes about God is that he put her here on earth . . . to love. What she does not like about God is "letting bad things happen. He can do things for people if he wants. We are always having to learn by our mistakes." For Kenzie, faith makes it possible for her to believe in God's goodness: "It's faith that helps me to understand the points and the levels, and what happens when I do something bad on the unit, that people are really trying to help me. Like Mary [a young woman with a disability] on the unit, we show faith when we tell her that we *believe* in her. Faith is believing in someone, and that you can do anything you want."

Kenzie is supposed to be going home in the coming week. In closing, Kenzie said that "it's faith that is going to get me back with my Mom."

Discovering Meaningful Patterns in Religious Narratives

The point of collecting and recording these religious narratives is to be educated by the young person as to their religious experiences, even in the midst of an institution. God gives children not only strength of character but enables them to discover some sense of meaning in what appears to be whirling chaos. Even these young people, who are living behind the walls of an institution where they are powerless, have had powerful religious experiences that give them hope in life.

In all three narratives, each adolescent describes, either generally or in great detail, an experience of God. Each adolescent also tells about his or her ongoing relationship with God that has been shaped, in large part, not only by the family, but by the very community of faith that the child has been brought up in over the years. What happened in the religious communities that the young people were raised in has strongly influenced how they interpret and understand what is now happening in their lives at the hospital.

In listening and reading these narratives, there are some lessons to be learned and confirmed about the power behind the call of stories:

The Narrative Shape of Life

The philosopher Alisdair MacIntyre discusses the purpose of narrative as providing a "unity of self."[12] The narrative of each person serves as a way of linking birth to life to death, as narrative beginning to middle to end. Narrative also reminds an individual that one is not an "isolated nuclei of consciousness" embedded in an historical context with deep implications for others set in the same context.[13] Quoting the philosopher Barbara Hardy, MacIntyre writes that "we dream in narrative, day-dream in narrative, remember, anticipate, hope, despair, believe, doubt, criticize, construct, learn, hate and love by narratives."[14]

What is revealed in these narratives is a certain unity, reasonableness, and logic that makes itself known as the young people tell their life stories. Yet these adolescents who, in the psychological and medical models, have been labeled and categorized anything from "schizophrenic" to "conduct disorder due to organicity," should not be able to understand the world with such logic. The assumption on the part of many professional health care workers is that these adolescents are not functioning with such a lucid, logical perspective on life; they are unable to rationally and logically "make sense" of the world.

Where did these young people take in the sacred stories that enable them to have some idea about what is happening in their lives? The soundness of each narrative may be attributed, directly or indirectly, to the experiences the child or adolescent had in a community of faith. Dale and Ben, growing up in the Jewish faith, envision God as spirit, void of a physical body, an orthodox worldview supported by the stories of the Hebrew Bible. Kenzie, African-American Baptist woman, who enjoys singing and shouting praise to God, reflects what is, in her church, a normal response to the presence of God. Her narrative reveals a certain unity with the community that she has been shaped and nurtured in, prior to institutional life.

The Lost Point Of The Story

The psychologist George Howard wrote that psychotherapy is an exercise in the repair of stories that are broken.[15] How one determines if a story is broken or whole is hard to judge. Perhaps another way of perceiving these life stories that have gone awry is by understanding that the goal or telos of their story is either vague or, in some cases, absent. Without this telos, the very direction and context of the story is obscured; disarray and confusion replace order and harmony.

Some of the young people do not know why they are living, or the meaning of life is lost on them. For now, all they want to do is get out of the hospital; they cannot see beyond the immediate future. Others have been misguided in the course of life-determining events existing beyond their control by someone who either misdirected them or left them to wander by themselves. Many of these young people come from families where they were sexually, physically, or psychologically abused by their elders or siblings. Their family story is riddled with abuse and lies; they cannot trust the very essence of the story or storytellers of their family for there is little that is good in the story. That is why many of these young people have lost the point of their whole story.

The philosopher Alisdair MacIntyre writes about the importance of a life story's telos. Without some kind of final telos, there cannot be any beginning to a quest. Some conception of the good is required by us which will enable us to understand the place of integrity in life.[16]

These adolescents believe that they are not at the end of their life story, only at the beginning, but they are not sure where they are to go after they get out of the institution, and, in some cases, why they should go. Many would rather stay in the life of a hospital unit than go back and face the complexities outside the highly structured institutional life.

The "good" in life for these adolescents is known only by their experience of God in the fellowship of the faith community in which they were raised. For some, God is the only good in their life. In knowing God's goodness, these young people also have an understanding of the other virtuous qualities of life, like "love" (Kenzie); the "Almighty" (Dale); and "Creator" (Ben).

The Power of the Sacred Story behind the Human Story

A most fascinating revelation in these narratives is the power of the sacred narrative of the adolescents' religious or faith community, even when the individual is in this hospital setting. Out of the abuse, hurt, and pain of being abandoned, there is still a glimmer of hope and faith in God in these lives. The beliefs of their religious communities, told in the stories and celebrated in the rituals of the faith community, are still present and at work in the lives of these children, shaping and nurturing their relational experience of God.

For example, take Ben's and Dale's narratives. Both of these young men perceive and experience God as "spirit" (Dale) and "mystery" (Ben). Portraying God as spirit and mystery is consistent with the portrayal of the leaders and prophets in the Hebrew Bible where God is continuously referred to as "spirit" and "mystery." God is not close enough to feel or touch; nevertheless, God is present in the silence and mystery of life.

Yet, the experience of God as mystery and spirit is not shared among those adolescents brought up in the Christian faith of the Baptist church. For Kenzie, a Baptist Christian, her experience of God is so immediate and surrounding that the palms of her hands are sweating when she prays sometimes, and she can even hear God's voice whispering to her during worship.

How these adolescents describe their experience of God in their narratives may be due, in large part, to the ritualistic celebrations in their respective communities of faith, and the sacred story that is central to the religious community's collective life. For the two young men who are Jewish, their experience of God as mysterious and silent is similar to how others in the Hebrew Bible, the sacred story of the Jewish faith, experienced God's presence. For other young people who are Christian, their experience of God is similar to the accounts of the young apostles as recorded in the book of the Acts of the Apostles and the occasion of Pentecost.

Implications of the Religious Experiences

In directing the adolescents' narratives on what may be described as religious or spiritual issues, the initial questions and answers revealed the depth of insight these young people have concerning ideas and impressions about life, church, synagogue, Jesus, and God. With all the participants, there was never a one-word reply to the question. Instead, the young people were eloquent and articulate in their explanations of complex theological issues.

In conclusion, there are some "lessons" to be learned from hearing and listening to these "teachers" of faith.

First, each child has had a different relationship or experience of God. No one story was quite like anyone else's story. While it would be easy to codify fragments of these stories, pointing to where they could fit in a "stages of faith" paradigm,[17] it is important to remember that each story, in its entirety, is unique, unlike anyone else's story that has been told before, or will ever be told again.

Second, the young people's verbal narration of their experiences of God makes sense. There is nothing too strange, unusual, or clinically pathological about their narratives, given the faith community they were shaped and nurtured in as younger children. Speaking from the immediate context of a residential treatment center for children and adolescents with emotional and behavioral problems, this is an important revelation. While one's ability to think reasonably or normally may be judged to be impaired in this setting, given certain psychological and educational tests in this clinical setting, the adolescents' narratives reveal an experience of God that is not too extreme or very unusual, given their unique backgrounds in their respective religious community.

Third, the sacred story's portrayal of God is clearly present in the lives of the adolescents' religious narratives. Prior to the position of "Director of Religious Life" and the "Religious Life Program" there was no emphasis on the religious or spiritual aspects of life in this institutional setting. There was no reinforcement of any religious community's sacred story or portrayal of God. Living in a secular institution with no access to their respective community of faith, it is impressive to see how the young person's portrayal of God reflects and corresponds with the very portrayal shared by specific religious communities.

The immediacy of God in the young people's religious narratives reveals how much their experience of God is part of their very beings. It is this experience of God that is, in the end, providing the telos in life that enables them to find a good way of living, whether in or outside the confines of an institution.

• • •

The following story is a fuller account of Kenzie's story, and her relationship with God. What is interesting about her relationship with God is how methodical and orderly it is compared to the seemingly scattered relationship other young people have with one another *and* with God.

13

Decently and in Order

Presbyterians like to think that they do things decently and in order in their church. If I have heard it once, I heard it and read it hundreds of times while attending Princeton Theological Seminary and sitting in numerous Presbytery meetings since graduation. In order to assure that there is widespread participation in the governing process, Presbyterians have constructed a polity of doing the business of the church around the notion of doing things "decently and in order."

Some of us need to be taught and learn about doing things decently and in order, given our propensity for being more scattered or fragmented than others. There are other people born with a natural inclination toward seeing orderliness not only life in their respective homes, schools, and churches, but life in general. This was true in the case of Kenzie, who is an African-American adolescent who had some emotional and behavioral disabilities, most likely due to abuse in the family at the hands of her father. Her ideas about God, home, family, and life in general had an order to it which would make most systematic theologians blush. These ideas were nurtured in the Baptist church in which she was raised, "though my mamma's going to a Jehovah's Witness meeting, which scares me for her." While some children and adolescents whom I have talked with have had some incomplete fragments of a theological imagination, Kenzie always impressed me because she was clear and precise about her understanding of God.

As was noted earlier in this book, Kenzie introduced herself to me in the unit's biweekly therapeutic community meeting, asking for an "injection of God's word" into her life's spiritual veins. Such imagination of anything dealing with God truly hooks a religious educator's attention. I asked her to spend some time telling me about her dynamic relationship with God. She had had a stressful day when I asked the question. Sitting in her room, not looking at me at first, and then, taking a deep breath, she said that if it would help me know God better, she would agree to talk. From that point on, I came to know God better through the life of Kenzie.

Kenzie is also a natural born teacher. She already has the presence and self-confidence to talk in front of some people, like her friends, and is able to follow and explain to others her logical thinking with remarkable clarity. And she already has down pat the talent and creative vision of using diagrams to explain herself better. For example, in my conversations with Kenzie, there were almost always visual aids for me to better understand what she was talking about. She naturally would pick up a pen, a color marker, or crayon on my desk, take out a clean white piece of paper, and begin to talk while drawing out a pictorial diagram of exactly what she was referring to, now and then pointing at the diagram to help clarify any questions I might have had. Meeting with Kenzie was an educational moment.

The first time she came into my office, she sat down at my desk and asked for a clean piece of paper. "What do you want me to draw?," she asked. I asked her to draw a picture of God, Jesus, and the Holy Spirit. "That's easy," and with that she drew God as a bird, "who goes everywhere and sees everything," and Jesus "the star that represents God. A star shines when you look at it. You learn more about God when you talk and think about it." And the Holy Spirit looked more like a white pillowcase than anything else, explaining that "a hood could go on anybody's head, and God is everywhere in the spirit."

The drawing lesson was not over yet, or so that was what Kenzie told me. Kenzie then took out another sheet of white paper and proceeded to draw an even more complicated diagram of heaven. It was then that I came to appreciate the orderliness of Kenzie's imagination. She kept telling me that she had thought about heaven long and hard, and the picture she drew made the best sense to her: to begin, on the left side, were sinners who needed to ask for forgiveness. If they did not ask for forgiveness and lied, then "you go straight to hell. If you tell the truth, then you go on to become one of God's children," located on the right side of the pictorial diagram. As for the priests: they go right to heaven. And in the upper portion of the picture is a hood (Holy Spirit), a star (Jesus Christ), and a bird (God).

. . .

The next time we got together to talk about God, Kenzie was feeling depressed, or as she described it, "having a down day." Her friends from her unit were being discharged, leaving Kenzie here by herself. Nonetheless, she has been organizing a Bible study with some other young girls on the unit. Kenzie, herself, is supposedly going to another placement in the coming month, and she is feeling apprehensive about leaving this place, which she understands and can control in part. The new placement is closer to home, and she is praying that she will be able to find friends at the new place, and soon.

To help her talk about her family, she drew a picture of the perfect house for her family. She drew a home with the usual rooms of kitchen, bathroom ("with a bathtub," she added), dining room, storage area, a TV room, and a pool table. Then each person had his or her own room: big brother, Mom, a separate room for her little sisters, and a room for her little brother, and her room that she would color "black, with pink polkadots." What was missing from this whole picture was Dad or Dad's room. The pain of Dad is still evident.

. . .

In our next meeting together, Kenzie was focused on the Bible, for she had had a Bible study that she ran on the unit. Suddenly, she was an authority on God, and was eager to talk about the Almighty. I asked her what her favorite Bible verse is, and from the top of her head, without losing a beat, she said "In the beginning there was Word and the Word was God . . . St. John chapter one, verse one." Taken aback by her memorization work I asked her what it meant to her: "It says that God was here first, and that he was the first word put on this earth, and he should be the first word to be remembered." She remembers learning this verse when she was seven years old, and she recalls this verse when "I'm in church for one, and if I'm in a situation where I don't know where to turn to." I asked her if that happened a lot? "Yeah," she replied.

When I asked her how she knew there was a God, she said that she knows God "because he knows me. And I know he knows me and I can talk to him . . . and he'll talk back to me in his own way." How does God talk to her? "He talks to me through other people." So Kenzie knows God through other people? "Yep, and I know him through the

Bible." Does God know Kenzie personally? "Yep. He sees me everyday, inside and out, upside and down and all around." When I asked her what does God think of Kenzie, she had to think about that. "She's intelligent, smart, has problems, but knows how to solve them, and knows how to stay out of trouble. A role model, a leader, smart, and that I'm going to make it somewhere." Why did God create Kenzie? "For an experiment . . . to see how much I could learn." Is she learning a lot? "Yep," was her reply, at first frowning, and then smiling, into a full giggle.

She confessed that sometimes she has taken abuse or ridicule on the unit or among other children at the hospital for her faith, like when she says a prayer before eating: "I thank the Lord before I eat dinner, and before other meals." Do they say anything? "No. They just look at me."

Regarding the church, Kenzie does not believe that you have to go every Sunday or Wednesday or even once a week:

> You should go whenever you feel like it. That means more than once a week or less than once a week. Put it into your schedule. But its very important that you don't have to go to church just to know God. That's what most people think that you have to go to church to know God, but that's not true. [You go to church because] it gives you more knowledge. At my church they ask that if you have people you want them to pray for or if you have a problem they will pray for you. And we will have special prayers.

In our next session, the theme was love. While I read from 1 Corinthians 13, Kenzie drew a series of red hearts on a piece of paper, filling the hearts with names of people whom she loves. According to Kenzie, love "is a gift from God, or yourself, or somebody else." Kenzie believes that one can live for a short period of time without love, "but they end up going down. They end up taking the opposite, wrong road," a road that is destructive; a road that she chooses not to go down.

We had begun to set up a regular pattern of visits, or lessons, when suddenly, within a matter of a week, I found out that Kenzie was going to be leaving for her new placement, a halfway home situation in a different city. When she came into my room, her affect was flat. She said, in a sullen fashion, "What are we going to be talking about?" I told her we could talk about leaving, and I gave her Psalm 139 to read to give her some security in knowing that God is going to watch over her, no matter where she goes in life: "If I ascend into heaven, Thou art there: If I make my bed in hell, Behold Thou art there. If I take the wings of the morning, and dwell in the uttermost parts of the sea; even there shall Thy hand lead me, and Thy right hand shall hold me."

She told me that the Psalm meant that "God's going to be with me no matter where I go." Do you agree? "Yep, I agree . . . [I sense God closest to me] all the time, whenever something went wrong. I always had a reason to do the right thing." When did God feel far away from her, or her from God? "Every time I went to the quiet room." The Quiet Room is a small room as big as a walk-in closet, with padded burlap walls, ceiling and floor, with one door in and out of the room, and a T.V. camera able to cover the entire room. Children are placed in the room when they are a danger to themselves or to the safety of others. Does God enter the quiet room with you? "Yes, he tries and talks to me while I'm in the quiet room, but I don't listen to him."

Kenzie believes that even in the midst of an institutional schedule and setting, God is present. She shared that her faith is stronger "because I saw I was getting better. When I first heard I was going to come here, I didn't want to come . . . I didn't think I was going to do good in here. I thought it was just another lock up, like any other one. I've been cared for here. [Care to me is] when you want to see the best happen to somebody [else]. And others want the best for me here."

• • •

In the letter to the Philippians, the Apostle Paul challenges and encourages other Christians not to get obsessed about the issues regarding law versus spirit (chapter 3:1–11), but to cherish the truth that, as a Christian, Christ Jesus has made him his own: "Beloved, I do not consider that I have made it my own; but this one thing I do: forgetting what lies behind and straining forward to what lies ahead, press on toward the goal for the prize of the heavenly call of God in Christ Jesus" (verses 13–15).

In many ways, Kenzie embodies this very passionate sentiment of the Apostle Paul, for this fragmented narrative is by a young woman who has known heartache and disappointment and yet still dares to yearn to be with God who somehow, some way, has let it be known that she is loved. This was borne out by Kenzie's ability to clearly articulate her faith in God, boldly challenging the presuppositions of the researcher, teaching the researcher and the reader about the nature of God, heaven, home, love, and faith.

How could she believe in God? What clamors for the attention of the reader and hearer of her life story is that this young girl began life as a victim of her own father's sexual problems. She has spent more time in institutional life than home life, going from one locked or double-locked facility to another one, discouraged when there was little help for her, and feeling abandoned and alone, separated from any family.

Given all the barriers that the world has thrown up in front of her, ceaselessly blocking her journey in life, the miracle is that there is still something within her character that calls her to go forward in life's adventure. Where did she get such resolve to make it in life? Given that she is still alive and doing more than merely surviving, Kenzie's story becomes one of moral courage, based solely upon her faith in a God who made it known to her in God's own way that she is God's own. Therefore, the question is not "How could she believe in God?" but "How could she *not* believe in God?" How else did she make it through to this place in her life's journey that she believes in pressing on with life, "toward the goal for the prize of the heavenly call of God in Christ Jesus."

14

The Religious Imagination of Disabled Children

Religious educators, theologians, and pastoral counselors have one thing in common: an interest in our imaginations, a direct result of being created in the image of God (Genesis 1). Imagination is somehow tied into creativity, for one cannot be creative without also being imaginative in the act of creating something new out of something old or already existing.

Imagination and creativity are characteristics of being human. And imagination and creativity know no label or category of a disabling condition, which is why even those considered as having a disability are still able to imagine and create. Instead of talking *about* imagination and creativity, it is better described in the context of a story than in a philosophical definition. Consider that the indomitable nature of the human imagination and creative faith may be found in these two stories. The first story involves George, a young boy of twelve, who has disheveled blonde hair and knees that are always scuffed up and dirty, for he wears shorts *all* the time. He reminds me of Charlie Brown's friend Pig Pen. While he is twelve years old chronologically, he acts more like a four- or five-year-old child emotionally, getting upset very easily when things do not come his way. He is also well known for "thinking" that he sees elves and fairies on the grounds of an institution where he lives away from his parents, in this interruption of his life.

But something interesting is happening in George's life. Since the first day that he found out that there was going to be a "pastor" working here, he wanted to build a church, a building not present on the hospital grounds. One day, with all seriousness, he stopped a group of children and an aide on the way back from the dining hall to inform them exactly *where* they were going to build the parking lot for the church near his unit. He has been intensely engaged with me about the act of building a church: "The hospital needs a church. When can we begin building it? Tomorrow?"

To help direct George's wonderful interest in the building project, I invited him to work with me in designing a church; this is a project that he takes on with great gusto. Over five months he has drawn me several churches on paper. Each church drawing, over a period of three weeks, looks more and more like a church. For example, the most recent church had a stained-glass window on one wall, doors in proportion to the walls of the building, a bell, and a cross on the top of the bell tower, "what Jesus was crucified on, right?," he asks. Next to the church is a park for "us kids to play at." Who lives in the church? "God," he replies, with a smile on his face.

The second story is that of Dennis. Dennis is Roman Catholic, thirteen years old, small for his age, with bright eyes, who was abused at home. When Dennis found out that George was drawing a picture of a church, he too wanted to get into the action. Said Dennis, "I'm a good artist . . . just ask anyone on the unit, and they'll tell you I'm real good." One night, he worked on a pencil drawing of a church. His artwork was full of great detail as he took it out the next day to tell me where the offices were of the church, the bookstore where they sold the candles, and the sanctuary, "with an organ, and a big cross with Jesus on it."

When I asked Dennis what he liked about church, he said it was "when we have that juice and that small wafer." To Dennis, God "is the man who created us." Jesus is the "son of the man who created us." When talking about Jesus, Dennis chose a blue pen to draw his picture of Jesus, careful with the details of Jesus' face. Dennis remembers the "big statue of Jesus on the cross, with a crown of thorns, and blood. He died for my sins, right?"

A Sensuist's Perception of the World

The sensuist, according to the writer Diane Ackerman, is "one who rejoices in sensory experiences."[1] What makes it possible for one to be sensuistic is that all human beings are sentient beings: we all have sense perceptions. She writes that we live "on the leash of our senses. Although they enlarge us, they also limit and restrain us, but how beautifully."[2]

As sentient beings, we understand and interpret the events of our lives and world by using our nonmaterial minds.[3] Yet the "mind," the entity of our conscious selves, is not isolated in the brain, but travels throughout the whole body on caravans of hormones and enzymes, making sense of the compounds of touch, taste, smell, hearing, and vision.[4]

By and through our human senses a sensorial impression from the midst of a religious community has been made upon the lives of these children with disabilities. Becoming conscious of that qualitative world or some aspect of it depends upon a skilled and intact sensory system, which apparently is true in these cases, as each individual was able to experience enough in the world in order to recompose or craft it in some understandable form. These sensory impressions have crafted and nurtured the child's ideas about where God should be worshiped (George), and imprinted Jesus' face on the heart and mind of a child (Dennis).

In order that these impressions made upon the child's life may be shared with others, what is needed is imagination, another one of those human traits that makes us different from other animals. Imagination is based upon the Latin word imago, meaning an image or representation. The root meaning is maintained in the verb "to imagine." When we talk about imagination, we refer to the capacity to conceive and express what is actually happening here and now, as well as what has been and could be in the future.[5]

Each child's imagination was working as they remembered and recalled something that impressed them during their participation in a church. More precisely, their eyes and ears captured some fragments of what they were experiencing in their respective religious communities. These young people are able to read the subtle nuances of the qualitative cues that constitute their environment. They are learning to distinguish and determine where the bell belongs on a church, and the exact look of Jesus' face that hangs on the cross in a young boy's church.

· · ·

What these two short narratives represent is the religious imagination at work in the lives of these young people who are disabled both in how they conceive of these images and impressions, and in how they communicate and express them in art. These imaginative works of art are religious in nature, for they reveal the child's capacity to be aware of God's presence in the midst of a religious community.[6]

How do we know about the religious imagination? Through the very artwork of the young people. The artwork becomes the mode of moral reflection; they are the displaying agency by which we, who also participate in the lives of these young people, can receive the impressions and communicate with the young people.[7] Given the right tools like a pencil and paper to write poetry, the creative space of an art room, the appropriate musical instruments, or a set of good colored pens and paper, the child will often attempt to make public that which is private. In essence, each child in the above stories had the capacity to externalize what was internal, making a shift from what was private to themselves in order to make it public and share it with others. Now the religious educator is "student" to the child teacher and is able to know the design of George's church, and Dennis's strikingly blue face of Jesus with piercing eyes. We see not only that these young people use creative, expressive tools for relaying their perceptions, but come to realize that these impressions have been, in some sense, locked up in the child's life for some time.

In living, working, learning, worshiping, and playing with disabled children and adolescents, like "mental retardation" or "behavioral disorders," a most powerful and vital path is revealed, showing what is commonly shared by all human beings: our imagination. In the context of communities of faith, it is our religious imagination that enables us to worship and learn together about God in our lives. It is when we are no longer spectators but become involved with one another that we find the pathway between our lives that enables us all, disabled and nondisabled alike, to communicate and *be with* one another.[8] It happens through our use of religious imagination in the midst of our faith communities.

Religious imagination is a powerful tool and is the essential link between those who are nondisabled and those whom society has labeled "disabled." In the next section, there will be further description of the role and function of religious imagination. This will be followed by reflection on the place of religious imagination in the lives of the disabled children. For it is through our imaginations that we may finally be able to see, hear, smell, feel, and celebrate God's presence in our midst.

Imagining Imagination

How do we describe the imagination? Imagination may be best understood in the context of a poem, story, or work of art. For example, the poet Richard Wilbur is talking about both mystery and imagination in this poem:

> All that we do
> Is touched with ocean, yet we remain
> On the shore of what we know.[9]

It is imagination, and the language of the imagination, that finally prompts us to wonder, to perceive what is normal in the abnormal, and discover where there is cosmos in the midst of chaos.

In discussing the word imagination, it may be helpful to consider that our imagination is multidimensional, involved in revealing that which is often hidden, made public in the context of community, through some concrete form of representation. First, in considering the multidimensionality of imagination, suppose that imagination has both a vertical and horizontal direction to it. The vertical direction enables us to lift our imaginative vision to new heights and to explore new depths, the very bedrock of our being. Imagination also has a horizontal direction to it as the imagination is keyed into perceiving the world around us, enabling us to take in and reflect upon those things that are meaningful to us. Imagination is keyed into perception. And it is this combination of imagination and perception that is involved in helping us in the present moment to finally connect the memories of the past while also envisioning the hope-filled future.[10]

Second, imagination is revelation. The educator John Dewey wrote that imagination is a vantage point of the future from which we can consider that which is lacking in the present or "now."[11] In wondering "what might be" and "what if only," our imaginations revitalize everyday living, which is the basic meaning of play, carnival, and recreation. Imagination is powerful, for it allows one to transcend the events of the "real world," where the person may be powerless, to a world of wonder, newness, and renewing sense of identity. For example, imagination is at work in George's mind as he imagines not only where the church that we are going to build may be placed on the campus, but in quite lucid thought, even knows where the parking lot and the playground should be situated.

Third, each person's imagination is tied into our tribal, social, or religious community and the rituals or traditions of these gatherings.[12] Having an imagination and thinking great, creative ideas is, in part, a private affair as the individual collects all manner of impressions from the surrounding life of the religious community in which one is raised. Yet to dream the thoughts, collecting the fragments of ideas and ways of representing our new thoughts, comes from life in community. And not to share them goes against what most of us so dearly want to do: to share our private images, what is internal, and to make them public and external, so that they may be appreciated and enjoyed by others. It is back in the traditions and rituals of our religious communities that a place or creative space is provided in which the individual may share his or her ideas. This was true for Dennis who, having attended a Catholic church as a child, remembers quite vividly the face of Jesus on the huge cross in the sanctuary. It was this impression of Jesus on the cross that caught Dennis's attentive imagination, later refigured in Dennis's drawing of the blue Jesus with such strong eyes looking straight into the eyes of the viewer.

Fourth, in order to give our imaginations a stage or empty canvas, and a means or tool for expression, human beings need some form of representation in order to share with others what they have imagined.[13] These forms of representation are the pictures, speech, dance, hand gestures, words, numbers, computer graphics, and songs that become the devices that enable us to share our internal, private impressions. These forms of representation not only make public what is private, but in doing so they become the essential means or mode of revelation and discovery for the imaginative person.

We witness the power of the forms of representation in the brown church that George drew, wondering what he is or is not going to include in the structure. Others who know George were impressed by the control of his line and how organized the whole structure was for a child who is well known for his scattered thoughts. We discover that there is order in what often appears disordered. Dennis's church reveals his ability not only to focus on the minute details of his church, but reveals his own, hidden talent for drawing.

What Is Revealed in the Imagination of These Stories?

Religious education is dependent upon the utilization of the human imagination. In the act of exploring and discovering the meaning of our experiences of God within the world and, more particularly, within our congregations, we are joined together on a journey of faith, which is guided by the sacred stories of our religious communities. The discovery and the understanding of our experience of God is facilitated by and through the imagination of our hearts and minds. We see the revealing power of the human imagination in a religious context and activity even in the lives of children who have been labeled as having "behavioral disorders."

In reflecting upon the stories, poetry, and artwork of these young people, there are three important lessons to be learned concerning the religious imagination of children with disabling conditions. To begin with, there is the sheer power of the private images that the young people have made public. Even in the midst of a secular institution, far from their family and friends, from congregations and parishes of their home communities, these young people have had an experience of God among a community of faith, which has made a deep impression upon their hearts and minds. They all believe that there is a caring, loving God in this otherwise abusive, disturbing, often chaotic world.

Next, these artistic and poetic images of the church, Jesus, and God enable the young people to transcend the well-managed therapeutic culture of a secular institution. The reader gets a sense of what could be construed as "normal" and "reasonable" in the lives of children who have been labeled and categorized as "abnormal." These images and ideas enable the young people to wonder, "What would happen if we *did* have a church here? What would it look like? What does Jesus look like to me? What would God want us to do in the midst of the foolish lies we live in?" These are powerful questions from these young minds and they may give them hope on the darker, more stressful, days of living in an institution.

Last, the common link or pathway of communication that has been missing in connecting the children who have been labeled "disabled" with others who are "nondisabled," *is* the imagination. A wall has often divided those with disabilities and those without disabilities in many religious education activities in congregations and parishes. Many of the curriculums used in congregations and parishes are created, developed, and written with a nondisabled child in mind as the audience and user, not the child with a behavioral disorder. With this bias, the very curriculum used in our congregations has created, unbeknownst to religious educators, a dividing wall between the two groups.

What do these two groups of children have in common? Our human imagination may be able to break down this wall and bring together the children, and adults, in religious education programs as we reflect upon the power of George's church and Dennis's blue Jesus. Creating activities that encourage an active use of our imagination, in a structured, group context, guided by the biblical stories as celebrated within the community, may be the "good news" that religious educators have needed to consider in making religious education programs and activities integrated.

As our imaginations and creative talents become engaged with each other, we now have a powerful way of exploring, discovering, and experiencing God's presence with us. By our imagination and creative talent, our faith in God is nurtured and shaped within the context of our congregations and personal relationships, revealing the high call of our human imagination in enabling us to experience God in our lives, and enabling God to experience us in the community of believers.

• • •

In the following two chapters, there is a continuation of George's story, or acts of creation, that he continues to work on, day and night. There is also Dennis's story, and his continual search for a place to rest his weary head and lonely heart in this world.

15

Pictures of God . . . at an Institution

People have been trying to some how, some way creatively and persuasively communicate with other people their thoughts and feelings of God, be it through the visual arts or written word. Rudolf Arnheim, a scholar fascinated by the interplay between art and psychology, wrote that visual images and verbal or written language are the two principal means by which human beings tell their life experiences.[1] However, the importance and use of these two means of expression and communication have not been held of equal worth in our society. More value has been placed upon those who have a better command of verbal language over those who see and express their vision of the world through visual images. Many artists are at a great disadvantage in this society when it comes to expressing themselves in a world of people who use only language to communicate with one another. What happens is a breakdown of communication, and often a discounting of the importance of visual images by the verbal language people.

John Dixon, professor emeritus of religion and art at the University of North Carolina-Chapel Hill, wrote about the "idolatry of words," which insert themselves into the "vast reverberating web of our common life, disturbing and shaping the interacting relations of our somatic life. Words are an indispensable instrument of being human as they undoubtedly serve to our becoming human. But our life is not in words."[2]

Dixon continues to discuss the primacy of the qualitative experiences of life, which shape and form us, over the idolatry of the written and verbal language:

Our life itself is lived physically in an intensely physical world. We do not live in a world of words but a world of sound and color, weight and textures, lines and surfaces, masses and volumes. The intricate network of our bones and muscles moves us through the volumes of our rooms. We fumble in the intimacy of closets and chests for the garments of our privacy and the costumes of our public selves.[3]

According to Dixon, the making of the work of art is basically a metaphoric activity, as one penetrates "into the secret life of things to find the bonds between them."[4] One could argue that God is also an artist, who engaged in a piece of metaphoric activity in the act of creating creation (Genesis 1). According to the Gospel of John, chapter 1, "In the beginning was the Word." Commentary writers understand that "Word" is translated from *logos*, which we read of as the living, breathing Word of God: "and the Word was with God, and the Word was God. He was in the beginning with God" (John 1:1–2). The living, breathing Word of God was, and still is and will be, Jesus Christ. And while some may read the Word of God as literally being the written word of God, others read it as the living Word, or life as in the life of Jesus Christ. Some theologians rightly argue that Jesus did not only verbally tell the story of God's love for creation while ministering on earth: Jesus *is* the sacred story of God's love for creation on earth.

One who seems to be able to imagine and understand Jesus as the living Word of God, and other theological issues of life better through one's imagination than verbal or written prose, is George. George is the twelve-year-old boy introduced in the preceeding chapter. He is labeled as having Attention Deficit/Hyperactivity Disorder (AD/HD), and is also developmentally delayed. He was born and raised in a southeastern state, and was admitted to the hospital two years ago. His short, dirty blonde hair looks as though it were tossed on the top of his head, and there always seem to be crumbs from his most recent meal somewhere around his mouth. If he had the opportunity, he would either be outside in the dirt and mud with his trucks and cars, or leafing through books and catalogues of pictures of truck and car models, vividly imagining and retelling the journeys of life on the open road as a trucker. For trucks and Jesus are the love of his life.

Throughout the year, most of my direct communication with George revolved around an ink pen or colorful markers and white paper. We drew, and sometimes constructed, a melange of things in my office: we talked and drew pictures of the nativity scene; we designed a collage or mural of the various parts of getting ready for the launch of a space shuttle; there is a self-portrait of George; and he designed many trucks of all sizes, shapes, and variety of uses, and a picture of the car from the hit movie, *Back to the Future*.

There was usually some narrative, or commentary to be more precise, associated with the drawings as we talked about what he was going to draw, and then discussed what he had drawn. Even with his relatively short attention span, I was always impressed by his intensity when it came to the task of drawing pictures and describing them to me. He was also not afraid to tell me what he thought, share his opinions freely with me, and not change his mind, no matter how hard I tried to convince him.

For example, there was the one incident when I tried to get him to draw me a picture of God. His response, "How?" Can you draw a picture of Jesus? "You can't see him, but he's around here somewhere." Finally, can you draw a church? "Yes!" And with that, he focused on that activity for over a good two minutes. When I asked if God was in the church, he said "Oh, yeah, but you can't see him. Only Jesus can." When I asked him if Jesus was here, George simply replied: "He was here a long time ago, before we were born."

One time, I tried to change his understanding of how Jesus died, but all to no avail. I felt more like a part of a Marx Brother act than anything else. I asked him what happened in Bethlehem: "They burned him." They burned him? Who was born in Bethlehem, I asked: "Jesus. But they burned him." "How did they burn him?," I asked "Or did they put him on . . . the cross." George responded: "A cross." Who died on a cross? "No, I think they burned him." I responded that they probably did not burn him, but put nails through his hands. "Why?," George asked. I told him, so that he would die. "Why?," George asked, again. I responded that people did not like him—or more importantly, what he was saying. There was a long pause while George thought about what I said. And then, sounding as if the people who crucified Jesus were part of the unit staff at the hospital, where there are retributive actions or what they call "consequences" if someone did something wrong on the unit, George simply stated: "They would have gotten consequences."

In another session, George brought in a project: we were going to create a collage of pictures George had cut out of the newspaper from the different parts of the space shuttle program near the hospital at Cape Canaveral. George cleared off the top of my desk, taking his arm across it and sweeping everything on to the floor . . . quickly. We cut out the parts of the shuttle program, gluing them onto a piece of white tag board, drawing in the buildings and all, and having some discussion of the program. I asked him where the space shuttle goes when it blasts off: "Space," he replied. Who lives in space? "Heaven." I rephrased the question again, "Who's up in heaven, George?" He told me, "God and Jesus," and went back to his project.

I never could get George to draw a picture of God, though I tried hard to persuade and cajole him to do so. His reply was always the same: "God's just there. You can't draw God." He could draw a picture of Jesus, and an angel; he could even draw a self portrait, but he would not and declared that he could not draw a picture of God.

However, George does not deny that God is present. One time, we spent the entire session constructing a Lego model of the church he wanted to design and build on the campus of this facility. We spent around thirty minutes on this project, and not once did his mind leave the task at hand: building a church. When I asked George where God was in this structure, he said that God comes in and out through the windows, talking with us, letting us know that he is there. He was not so worried about God, though, as he was about where all the people were going to fit who wanted to be with God. He told me the next time that we worked on the structure we would have to work on the inside space so that all the people who wanted to come to church could sit down. He thought we needed more furniture, "somewhere for the people to sit as they talked and sat with God!" he said emphatically, checking the last brick of Lego that he put in place.

It was during one of George's truck drawing moments when he said something that made me stop and think about the wisdom in this young artist's pictures and mind: George had been playing throughout the school day with his trucks, as well as leafing through the numerous catalogues in his room, filled with one model truck after another. In he came to my office, quickly sat at my desk, cleared it off in his inimitable style, took out paper and pen, and started drawing a truck. But this was not to be *any* truck: this was a Christian truck, which had a small cross carefully drawn on the door, and on the building located at the back end of the truck. Why did he put a church on the back of the truck? "Because we have to take God's Good News out to the people some way, so we'll put it on the back of the truck." With George at the wheel of the truck, he is off to spread the good news. I had little else to ask, and just marveled at his answers for the rest of the day. I asked him who loves him, and he said calmly, "Mom, Dad, and God," and then smiled, dashing out of my room and back to the classroom.

We have had many opportunities to draw and glue pictures together. I have a creative truck on top of the bookshelf in my office. It is made out of empty toilet paper rolls for wheels and the bottom of a tissue box that he made on the unit, being held together by a wish, a prayer, and too little glue. George made the entire truck with only the picture of the truck in his mind. He did not have any model in front of him, and had little help from the staff on the unit. He called me over to his door one evening, asked me to stay at the doorway to his room, close my eyes, and hold out my hands. Into my hands he put this creation, and then stood back, telling me to "open your eyes now." With my "ahhh" of deep appreciation for the gift came a yelp of great joy from George. "Do you know what it is? Do you know what it is?" he said jumping up and down in place; "It's a truck for Jesus! For Jesus! For Jesus!" I hugged him for the beloved gift for Jesus, this "truck for Jesus," and he told me to put it on my bookshelf for others to see. I also have a picture of his Christian Christmas tree truck, with a tree in the back, and numerous other vehicular drawings, all designed by the artful George.

What these drawings have become is part of a larger display of pictures in an institutional exhibition by not only George, but along with others as well who have a better idea of what they are talking about when they can either capture it in the poetic rhythm of the language, or in the simple lines on a piece of paper. These pictures are more than artful scribbles. Such artwork is a form of communication that I am struggling to understand and better appreciate, for I barely get ahold of one child's style and tool of expression before another child comes to me with a different one, as each child is unique in their method of sharing their vision or story of God. No picture of God, Jesus Christ, or the Holy Spirit is the same, which is as it should be. For while we may all attest to our common experience of the essence of God in the midst of our congregations and parishes during worship, filled with uplifting congregational singing, bright banners, stunning stained-glass windows, and strong whiffs of incense, God is doing something quite creative in us: God honors the creation by inspiring us to envision God and relate to God through artistic or metaphorical images. Perhaps this explains in part why we each have a different vision of God: even though we confess that there is but one God who made heaven and earth, each of us have come to be in relationship with God in such unique ways that stymie and enhance our collective imagination. Signs of God's unique representational relationship with us is borne out in the images we have of the Trinity, which then allows us to express our faith not only in our own words, but by our very vision of who is God.

What George has done is tried to capture in his imaginative drawings something of the essence of God, as he learned about God while playing on the pews during worship in a small church in Tennessee. However, these are more than simple drawings of a disabled child: these are invaluable drawings of one of God's people, who is yearning to understand better and capture God in his mind's eye. This is the God whom George is so excited about that he has to take the church to the people in order to tell them the Good News: that God loves us.

16

The Fragmented Puzzle

One of the more frustrating experiences of life, which sometimes requires more patience than Job and the communion of saints combined, is an incomplete puzzle. When looking at puzzles, there is something that calls for completeness and draws one to finish it. Be it a child's small, colorful wooden puzzle, a complicated fifteen-hundred-piece adult jigsaw puzzle, or the intense crossword puzzles in the back of the *New York Times Magazine* section on Sundays, there is something that makes us feel out of whack and off-balance until the puzzle pieces find their proper resting place in the context of the larger puzzle.

Children with behavioral, emotional, and developmental disabilities are like puzzle pieces. However, their puzzle pieces are more dangerous and poisonous to the touch, for they have been broken by the agonizing abuse, the incestuous, tormented relationships of family and neighborhood life gone awry. They are living, brittle, sharp, puzzle pieces that, for the time being, make no sense and have no readily defined pattern to them. These children come to us with their painfully fragmented, incomplete, fractured lives, wanting to be made whole, or to explain to them ways of making or giving sense to their inner sense of brokenness. They are hurting and are often in great pain. It is this pain that makes them violently lash out and destroy others out of their own sense of being destroyed. They come to health service professionals, be it in a psychiatric institution, residential treatment center, or community mental health center in a city, barely holding onto the innumerable bits and pieces of their life stories that no longer make any sense to them or to their families. In the case of these children, they are not necessarily missing the puzzle pieces of life: they are lost as to how all these pieces fit together within a larger framework. They need to begin with a table, a bed, or stable floor to sit upon, rest, eat, gather their energy together, get their bearings, in order to start, with the help of others, the arduous yet much needed task of piecing together their fractured life.

This scattered sense of self is reflected in twelve-year-old Dennis. Like many of the children at the hospital, Dennis is looking for a place to sit down, and a caring community of a friend or two to join him in putting down these puzzle pieces in a way that they begin to make some sense to him. This is easier to write or to say than to do: Dennis will need a community of friends to constantly aid and encourage him in bringing out his puzzle pieces that have hurt him in the past. The task will challenge the other person, the friend, to believe in Dennis especially when he does not believe in himself, which is often these days. While Dennis calls for friends to help, at the same time he pushes against friends when they come too close to him, truly testing them to see how good and solid the friendship is. Some psychologists call this a double-bind situation. Whatever one wants to call it, in doing so, Dennis demands much of his friends.

Dennis hunted me down because he wanted to have a certified hospital "volunteer" whom he could call his own. Within the hospital staff, people could participate in a volunteer program for the children, which gave them permission to take children off the units and campus, and to other parts of the neighboring community. As the Director of Religious Life, I was permitted to take children out to church, to see a currently running film, to buy some much needed clothes, and other sundry things. Dennis claimed that he was the only one on the unit among the children who did not have a volunteer, which was not exactly true, but it sounded good and got my attention.

One of the first times we went for a walk around the campus, Dennis was easy to talk with, eager to share some of his past history. As was shared in an earlier chapter, Dennis remembers attending Mass at the neighborhood Roman Catholic church where he grew up. The image of Jesus nailed on the cross in the front of the church sanctuary made such an impression upon Dennis that this one image is his primary way of understanding and knowing God in Christ.

The next time we got together to walk and talk, Dennis shared with me where he or members of his family have lived. Our discussion became more personal. As I had lived in Oregon and Washington,

Dennis's mother had lived in California and Arizona, "and perhaps Oregon, too," he shared. We both agreed that while snow is fun to look at, we are both glad to be in Florida come the winter months.

His mother lives and works in the Miami area. The reason that Dennis left his mother in Miami is because of the drug traffic that he had become involved in with some gang in the area. Dennis was one of the young couriers who would help deliver supplies and recruit other young children to the drug traffic in the area. He was a young drug runner before he was ten years old.

I met Dennis outside the unit the next time we met. He was hot and a bit winded after an enthusiastic game of kick-the-can with other children from the unit. After cooling off a bit, he asked to come to my office to talk some more "about God and stuff."

When we got to my office, Dennis was eager to draw some more, for he sees himself as an artist, "the best on the unit." During our time together, Dennis drew his vision of heaven, which would be a house for all the other children on his unit. His house would include a video arcade, with a "Chip 'N Dale" machine. There would be a kitchen with lots of food because "I like a lot of stuff." I would have couches, and special cabinets "in case there's ever a tornado." The house is big, able to sleep fifty people, with one animal: his dog, Bear. Dennis told me that Jesus probably has a dog, but that the angels probably have to watch over it. Dennis is sure that God made dogs "to protect people, and to have a friend when someone [close] dies." Why did God make Dennis? "To draw and ride bikes . . . and swim fast." Finally, at this house there would be a "quick sports car," and plenty of ice cream in the freezer. What makes him happiest in thinking about this house is that it is outside the hospital.

Prior to Christmas, Dennis and I had some time together to talk about the holiday and what it meant to him: "Care, love, giving . . . not giving, sharing." Christmas is not just *an* important time to Dennis, but *the* most important time, because "Jesus is born then," and there is the possibility that Dennis will have some time with his mother.

I then asked Dennis what he thought about Jesus lately, and he said "I don't know him." I asked him if he meant Jesus? He replied, "I don't know him." He answered the same for God and the Holy Spirit.

Interested in these responses, I tried to find out exactly what he was suggesting: Do you want to know God, I asked? "I do, but I don't know." Dennis is not smiling, and he is not trying to cover up anything:

he is being truly honest with me about his faith. I backtrack and ask him what he wanted from Santa Claus and if he believed in Santa: "A pair of Reeboks, and I do believe in Santa." Do you really, I asked? "Yes. He's a Spirit." I went deeper: "Why do you believe in Santa and not Jesus?" To which he replied "I do believe in Jesus. Why do you say that?" Now I was confused. He then clarified that he *believes* in Jesus, but he does not know Jesus: "You know me. You see me. You hear me. I don't hear God. I don't see Him. I believe in Jesus." I then asked that if he cannot see Jesus, how does he know there is a Jesus, and whether or not he really believed in Jesus. Dennis was adamant with me: "I believe in Jesus."

Interested in continuing this dialogue, I asked Dennis if he was going to get involved with the drug gangs again when he goes home. He declared he is not going to. Instead, Dennis told me that he is going to church every Sunday. I nonchalantly then inquire as to what he would give the baby Jesus as a gift on Christmas morning if he was in Bethlehem. Dennis paused, smiled, and said "It's embarrassing to say so . . . but my heart." What's in Dennis' heart? "Love."

• • •

Dennis has many fragmented puzzle pieces that do not come together easily. Unlike many of the other children's stories that I have been a part of, where there was a sense of wholeness and symmetry to their story, Dennis was a real challenge to me. He ran hot and cold all the time. For example, on some days he would see me in the hallway and pester, if not beg me, for a chance to talk about God in my office. However, when he would sit down in my rocking chair or behind my desk, he would then close down, build a wall between us, and sometimes not talk at all, especially about God. At a few points in our sessions, he would ask why I was taping him, or why did he have to draw another picture, or say anything else about God. Now and then, I was completely ignored by Dennis in the halls of the schools or other parts of the campus, no longer serving some purpose in his goal of survival in the institutional unit.

Being with Dennis has not been easy but tricky. I am never sure where he is coming from, and how or where to meet him in terms of his view of God and life. At some points, his puzzle pieces appeared round and smooth to the touch, manageable, filled with great insights into himself and the nature of God and he was a delight to be with.

Yet at other times, the ends and edges were so sharp I would almost feel cut by his caustic remarks and rejection of help. Sometimes Dennis acknowledged that he needed God, and at other times he said that there was no need for God in his life.

In sharing life's journey with Dennis, I again turned to Psalm 139, which describes in rich examples the "inescapable God" (New Revised Standard Version of the Bible). In turning to Psalm 139 I have sought some solace and comfort in the belief that, regardless of the fragmented condition of these children and the hurt they self inflict and their abusive treatment of friends, they too were formed and knitted together in their mother's womb by a loving God. While Dennis, and a host of the other children whom I have come to know and love at this hospital, may think that they are hidden from God's presence, the Psalmist understands the omnipresence of God: whether one ascends to heaven, makes a bed in Sheol, takes the wings of the morning and settles at the farthest limits of the sea, or tries to hide in a unit of twenty-five children with various disabling conditions at a secular psychiatric facility, God's presence is even there, day and night. It is this knowledge, this guarantee of a limitless, unbounded love, reiterated time and again by a community of believers that will provide children like Dennis with the hope-filled relief of being settled down, having spread out their puzzle pieces, and beginning the necessary task of placing them together.

17

Holy Surprises

In a hospital for children and teenagers with disabling conditions, it is a safe bet that kids will say and do the most surprising and unexpected things. While the worst-case scenarios that people imagine seldom come to fruition, the adults "in charge" learn to revise their estimates of what is, after all, possible.

Might I tell some more stories?

The first story belongs to Sal. Sal is a hugger. She will, if given a chance, throw herself upon you, with all her eighty pounds of freckles, strawberry blonde hair, and childhood kinetic energy, as she simultaneously asks *whether* she can hug you. Sal is also labeled mentally retarded and hyperactive; she also has a speech impediment. But this does not interfere with her relationship with God and her friends and family.

In working with Sal there have been a lot of surprises. She has been at the institution for over two years. In the last few weeks now, when I have been teaching the youngsters songs and Bible stories, Sal has eagerly joined in the singing and storytelling, sitting close to me and touching the guitar, feeling the vibration through the wooden panels. One day, when I started to sing "Jesus loves me this I know," Sal suddenly sat straight up, started bouncing up and down, and raised both hands high over her head. "I know that song," she said. "Start it again," she squealed in her delight at knowing the song. And singing it again, Sal revealed for the whole circle of staff and children that she knew the hand signs for the entire song. We were all amazed, staff and children alike. What is remarkable is that she had to have learned this song before she came to the hospital, because her speech therapist did not teach her the hand gestures, nor did I; and she had never sung that song for us before. For over two years, Sal has known that song far better than we could have imagined, could have thought . . . well, possible. Finishing her encore with a big, knowing grin, she said "I love that song. It's one of my favorites. Can we sing it again?"

Sal had more than one surprise for us. Another surprise occurred while reading and acting out the story of *Toddlecreek Post Office* by Uri Shulevitz.[1] The basic plot? Toddlecreek Post Office is presided over by Vernon Stamps. It is a place where friends could gather to pass the time in conversation. Even dogs were welcome here to take their daily rests. And the warm, comfortable routine continues each day until something horrible happens to the gathering in the post office.

After reading and acting out the story, I usually gather the children around me, and we talk about its meaning. Noting all the people, and animals, gathering at the post office, I asked the children what was happening there, hoping that they understood that the Post Office had become a community. Sal raised her hand and simply answered: "It was now a home." Toddlecreek post office was now a home, a family. She smiled at me, pleased with her response, and I smiled back.

My second story belongs to Jerry. Strong and tall, no fat and all muscles, Jerry was raised in one of the inner cities of the northeast. He has a history of letting his raging anger get control of his life and harming those who are with him. Soon after he got here, Jerry caught some staff off guard with his excitement in learning that there was a pastor at the hospital. Jerry was anxious to meet with me, because he had something to talk to Jesus about: girls. He said, "I'm lusting in my heart, and I know I need to talk to Jesus about it." And the only way he knew to reach God was through prayer. Much to the surprise of the staff, he asked for permission to call together a weekly prayer group on the unit!

Since our initial meeting, every Monday night Jerry calls together two or three of his friends on the unit. I join them, and we join in singing, reading from the book of Psalms, and praying. Jerry has now found the community he needed to pray that Jesus would cleanse his heart and bring peace to his mind as he begins to look for a young woman to whom he can be truly faithful for the rest of his life. The last time I met with Jerry, he had persuaded half his unit, seven young men, to join us in a time of singing, praying, and sharing.

Finally, meet Max: Max has a smile that can melt most people's hearts. It is a smile that caught my attention when I first began working on his unit. He has been at the hospital for quite some time, having his problems when he *is not* smiling—losing his temper at home in an angry, violent fashion. Recently, on the day when the nation celebrated Martin Luther King, Jr.'s, birthday, Max surprised the staff with a "rap" poem that he wrote during his spare time. In preparing for the community gathering in memory of Martin Luther King, Jr., Max read this rap:

> Martin Luther King was a good old man.
> He helped out black folks as best he can.
> He had a dream:
> One day this nation would come together,
>   And join hands.
> Martin Luther King, civil rights he preached.

In each of these stories—with their distinctive twists—something surprising about youngsters with disabilities, and about hospital life, is being revealed. For these stories suggest paradox. Normal stories become surprises because of the very ethos of the hospital setting where they are lived out. For the hospital ethos reinforces the idea that these youngsters are abnormal, disabled, and limited in their abilities to make it in the "normal" world.

The marked difference between the ethos of our hospital and the ethos of a natural setting—a church, a home, or a school—is the important shift in basic assumptions. In an institution, especially for youngsters with behavior disorders and mental retardation, children so labeled are *expected* to act disabled. Everything that the child does is given meaning by the understanding that no matter how aberrant the behavior may be, such inappropriate behavior is now normative in the clinician's view of the disabled child. The professional and the parent come to *expect* the child who has been labeled disabled to be different than "normal" children in the world.

This devaluation of the child is exactly what makes my stories of the ordinary take on the aura of the extraordinary. In the institutional setting, what would be considered "normative" outside the institution is now considered unexpected. The care giver is caught off guard by the normal response, because it is occurring in a setting where disabled assumptions color the professional's understanding of and relationship with the child. My stories, indeed, are holy surprises; for these surprising responses and events happen when the children are together as a community in the name of God in Christ.

Learning about life through paradox, where the ordinary becomes the vehicle for revealing the extraordinary, is not a new phenomenon for Christians. In the Gospels, God often takes that which is ordinary and makes it extraordinary: a dirty manger becomes a cradle for the Son of God; a donkey ride into Jerusalem becomes a hero's welcome; ordinary bread and wine at Passover became a sacramental holy feast.

Remember the story of the feeding of the five thousand (you'll find it in John 6:9–14)? Here a young boy has brought his lunch of five barley loaves and two fish to eat while listening to Jesus. Jesus uses this boy's simple, ordinary meal and performs a miracle that stuns the large and festive crowd. More than anyone imagined *possible* were fed from this paltry offering of average fare. The barley bread was peasant food—barley was used to feed animals, and only the poor used it for their own bread. The fish were probably small and pickled, making up for the dry bread. Jesus, taking the bread of the poor and the pickled fish, blessed and broke it, shared it with others. And there were twelve baskets of food left over. A holy surprise.

Whether one believes that the bread and fish truly were multiplied, or that the very act of Jesus's sharing food prompted others less generous to share until all were full, is worth exploring. But far more important is that we understand the interaction between Jesus and the boy. Jesus saw the lad, and in looking at the bread and fish he brought to this gathering, Jesus took the food the young lad had, and found in the mundane the makings of a miracle. The five ordinary loaves of bread and two ordinary fish became the necessary substance for this extraordinary event where five thousand were fed. Those gathered said, "This is indeed the prophet who is to come into the world" (John 6:14).

Like the young lad with the bread and fish, these "disabled" children come as they are to this institution, and come with a long list of behavioral and medical problems that challenge and test the most patient and caring people among the staff. And each child comes to the religious activities at the hospital just as he or she happens to be, sometimes emotionally overwrought about what was said in a therapy session, sometimes tired from a day at school. Yet in these activities, at those times and in that space where it is "permitted" to talk and share our lives with God, the surprising and *extra*ordinary happens. What comes forth out of the child is beautiful, innocent, good, and true. These characteristics are given a chance to be spontaneously expressed in an otherwise controlled and predictable setting. Sal shares her love of Jesus and knowledge of a song and its hand gestures for the first time, much to our amazement. Angry Jerry reveals his deep, child-like love for Jesus, his concerns about his lust for the young women, and his ability to forgive others in hopes that they will forgive him for his faults. And Max, who has never shown the initiative to write, let alone compose a rap, is encouraged by our special gathering to reveal a deep admiration for his hero, Martin Luther King, Jr.

And we, who witness these events, are truly surprised and taken aback by such moments, surprised by God in the lives of these young-sters. God in Christ takes what these children have in the midst of these communal gatherings. Though it may be as simple as bread and fish, not very much in the perception of others, it is enough to reveal the loving and caring presence of God in the lives of these young people. A holy surprise, indeed.

18

George's Encounter with the Lord: An Adventure[1]

Religious educators, Jewish and Christian alike, are fascinated both by what we know of God and how we learn it. The educator Parker Palmer asks a related question: How do children and adults come to know God and be known by God?

For the most part, religious educators have assumed that this journey, the eternal dialogue of knowing and being known by God, is a conscious act that is facilitated by either verbal or written activities (on the intellectual side), or by tangible and concrete experiences (on the physical side). They carefully craft Sunday school curriculum filled with activities for children and adults alike that keep people's hands active, stimulates their spirits, and in most cases, focuses primarily on their minds. Often, religious educators focus so much on the intellectual that it appears to some that we are playing mind games with knowledge of God. More than once, congregations have lost the point of the pastor's sermon when it digresses into an analysis of the exact New Testament Greek vocabulary for abstract concepts—justification, sanctification, and eschatology.

Religious educators have a definite, concrete setting in mind in constructing their activities, usually Sunday school classrooms, youth group meeting rooms, and family homes. Current curriculum stresses semicontrolled, experiential activities and small group discussions that become the catalyst by which students may learn something about the nature of God—or so we hope.

In spite of our carefully crafted words and abstractions, all with the goal of talking about (and around) the nature of God, we sometimes lose sight of God. While we think we know how to shape and nurture children and adults in the faith, within our neatly constructed curricula, we are shocked when, out of nowhere a door is suddenly opened for the Lord to come into our lives. All of a sudden, without warning, God can crash through our neatly constructed categories defining, within simplified limits, the ways of learning about the Almighty. In breaking our models, God is once again truly the innovative God. The novelist Graham Greene once said that there are moments in life when a door suddenly opens and lets the future in. That future, for Christians, is the Lord.

Such a radical door was recently opened wide in the still unfolding story of George. The episode in this story that needs our focus here concerns George himself, his mother, and the church.

George has the body of a nineteen-year-old boy, and a mind of . . . well, that's the issue. No one is quite sure at this time. Up to a few months ago, George, who is rather normal in physical appearance, was perceived by his family to have the mental age of a toddler. George has been labeled autistic, meaning that he has experienced a disorder of development. Uta Frith, an expert in autism, writes that "in adulthood, mental development is not only distorted and delayed, but if [life's] aim is maturity, then this aim is never reached . . . Existence remains curiously restricted and abnormal."[2] Like other young people with autism, George has his own self-stimulating behavior. For example, he repeatedly says "record player, record player," tapping his teeth when anxious, and rocking in place.

Unbeknownst to George's mother, her parents, and the church they are attending, George had been watching and listening to most everything in life that has been occurring around him and to him, as well as what he has done to others for the past nineteen years. Only recently, in the last few months, the hospital's speech pathologist who works with George has discovered that he not only can type in a hunt and peck manner, but when he is given the freedom to type, he has quite a bit to tell the world. For inside the outer shell and simplistic childlike actions of someone who acts more or less like a toddler, there is a young man who is suddenly finding a way to communicate with the world. And what he is finally telling the world with great urgency is what he has been thinking, feeling, and experiencing in life. He has discovered that he is, indeed, a person with ideals and opinions and attitudes, and, not surprisingly, faith.

The means by which George was freed from the prison of his special bodily limits and distorted actions is a new approach for people with autistic behavior: facilitated communication. This new method is similar to the old hunt and peck method of typing. What is different is that the typing is done on a handheld portable computer with a little ticker tape that produces the messages. Some health service providers see it as a quill of sorts, a pen. The technique is simple. Someone holds the autistic person's hand, elbow, or shoulder, and those with autism have the physical support needed to type and communicate what they think and feel on small computers. George, having memorized the keyboard, is even able to type while looking away from the board.

Needless to say, this innovation radically transformed the relationships that everyone—family, teachers, speech pathologist, members of his church—had with George. On the one hand, everyone is thrilled that the child who could never express his thoughts and emotions except through simple, repetitious gestures, now has quite a bit to say to, and about, the world around him. On the other hand, this is an awkward time as George discovers the power of language to both build healthy relationships, and to destroy them, sometimes with just one word. George now has the capacity to tell the truth, as well as to lie; the chance to tell of beautiful things, as well as to reveal his ugly thoughts; the ability to share tender feelings of love, as well as to turn people off with messages of hate.

There are days of frustration when George appears to be trying to get out everything that he has bottled up and experienced for the past nineteen years. His great angst can leave his hand motionless and silent as it hovers over the keyboard. Facilitated communication gives George more than a voice, a simple means of expression. It provides him an opportunity to discover who he is among others. In discovering his identity, he is finding his place in his family, in the world, and in God.

For the religious educator, one of the fascinating developments in this unfolding story of George's secret life as a nineteen-year-old is that he claims to be a Christian. And what is intriguing about this claim is that George has never seriously been talked to or treated as a young man of faith by anyone in the church, including his immediate family.

Everyone thought that George was autistic. No one talked to him directly about matters of faith, discussing the details of justification and sanctification, or the meaning of baptism. And George, given the choice of being with the young people of the church or the preschool class, would play with the preschoolers. He has never been involved in youth group meetings, Sunday school activities, or Bible studies, because the church does not have them. His mother said that George has mainly stayed by her side during worship, fellowship hour, and her Bible study.

However, even with the facade of not being engaged with what is happening, George has been taking in all the messages and gestures around him. Despite his seeming inattention and detachment, George has been watching and listening, feeling and sensing, a great deal indeed. And despite the church's best efforts *not* to treat him as a believing member, George still believes in Jesus Christ as his Lord and Savior.

The evidence of George's faith has been revealed in the following sessions. George typed all the statements in response to talks we had over a period of two months. A speech pathologist was in the room as well, using facilitated communication with George.

Session One

One day, George started to really type messages directed to his mother, telling her things that were on his mind: "You used to tell me I was a calm boy because I did nothing. I can talk now . . . I have changed." His mother said that she feels that she has missed out by not being able to talk with George, and George offers to her some hope: "Let me type; I can type with you." While his mother prays that he will talk someday, George responds with "I do not need to talk; I know God wants me to type."

Session Two

When asked today if he is a Christian, he said "yes." His favorite song at church is "Jesus is Lord." It is either Saul or Ray who leads the music in church. His mother said it was Ray; Saul leads the Bible study she takes George to. His mother is amazed. When asked what he likes most about Christ, George said: "I like most that God gave me life."

When asked what he thinks of facilitated communication, he typed "facilitated communication is great. Now I can talk." When he was asked if he wants to stop, he said "no, I want to tell my Mom that I love her very much because she loves the Lord."

Session Three

George was asked if he knew what baptism in water means. "It means that you believe in God; that you love Jesus." When asked if he prays, George said that he prays "by myself to the Lord." I asked him what his gift was in the body of Christ. His answer? "The ear"—because he listens to everyone and, up to this point, has not had occasion to talk with or to others.

Session Four

One of the striking statements of this session came out of an ongoing issue regarding George's typing and using facilitated communication with his mother. He said that there is "something that makes communication work between two people: trust." While he trusts the speech pathologist, he does not always trust his mother.

Session Five

Today George made it clear that his mother must be patient with him. He is frustrated that he and his mom cannot type together, because "we have so much to say to each other now that I can type." This is especially hard on his mother, who has waited years to talk *with* her son, not *at* him; to pray *with* her child, and not *for* him. Her frustration with facilitated communication is palpable at times.

Session Six

George had had a good day in school. He was willing to talk about silly as well as serious things, including that he likes to read *Good Housekeeping* and *Ladies Home Journal*.

When George was asked if he would like to read the Bible, he said that "yes, I would like to read the Bible." In talking about typing with his mother, he spontaneously said "I love the Lord," and that he would like to type with Dr. Brett (the author).

· · ·

"George's Encounter with the Lord: An Adventure" is a fitting title for this time in George's life, for this is exactly what has been occurring. Many things have dramatically changed for George since he has learned to communicate with others. He can now share, with the help of facilitated communication, his thoughts and feelings. Before, people would try to read and understand what he was conveying with his ritual behavior of tapping his teeth and "record player" chant. Now a door has been constructed in the wall of autism that had once separated George from the rest of the world. George has opened the door to life, and a new adventure has begun for him, his family, his school, and the church that he is an integral part of.

This ability to communicate has had a direct impact upon George's idea of who he is: his very identity has changed. From the vantage point of the outsider, the label "autistic," which for nineteen years has hung around his neck as a sign for others to see, seems misplaced and outdated. The label no longer conveys the rich complexity of who George is; it falls miserably short of capturing the life that George experiences. From what George types, we read that he has definite ideas and opinions about what is going on in his life. For nineteen years, unless he visibly became upset or happy, others would decide what he would wear, what he would listen to on the record player, whether or not he would see TV, even which restaurant he liked most. Now he has the ability to make his own choices, and tell others what he has decided.

Yet George is not only finding out what it means to be "George." The church he and his mother attend are also finding out what it means for George to be a Christian and believe in the Lord Jesus as his Savior. George also knows *whose* he is. While he is not always sure about some aspects of his life, like whether he likes pizza or hamburgers the most, George consistently says he loves Jesus and is one of God's children.

What is amazing is how he learned that he is loved by God. George's story places a distinctive question mark on the existing theories of religious education, which address how we know God and how God knows us. It is just possible that human beings, God's creatures, may also learn of God by more than words written and spoken about God. There may be a multitude of ways yet unexplored and unnamed by religious educators through which God's children come to know Jesus Christ, including through facilitated communication. God may come to us through the most creative and unexpected means, and through the simplest gestures of faith, hope, and love, experienced in the community of Christ.

George's encounter with the Lord, and with life, has taken an unexpected turn in the journey of faith; a turn that reveals a new way of knowing and loving God and others. It has not been an easy time for his family who, for nineteen years, have been treating George as a toddler. God is doing something innovative and different once again, teaching us all that we have much to learn, ourselves, about the gracious act of knowing and being known by God.

19

It Happened Around the Church

Like a classic mystery, an unsolved whodunit, there is evidence of some godly play in the young lives of children with behavioral and emotional problems at the hospital where I work. Something happened at some time in the lives of these young people, before they entered the double-locked doors of the institution, which made an indelible impression upon their hearts and minds. Now, in the presence of God, in certain places, in the company of believers engaged in "unusual" activities, comes forth the strangest and most peculiar responses from the disabled children gathered together to sing, read the Bible, and pray: faithful responses.

Jonah

Consider these "cases" as evidence of the suspicious happenings. The first case concerns Jonah. Jonah is a tall, heavyset young man of fifteen, who has been labeled mentally retarded, has a physical impairment due to epilepsy, and has a speech impediment. When looking at Jonah's simple smile, contorted expressions, and his awkward walking shuffle, one wonders what is going on in his mind. One week, while I was leading religious story time on his unit, Jonah suddenly wanted to join in the activities. The other young people and I welcomed him with open arms. He was delighted to come, smiling as he awkwardly shuffled into the room. The first sign of "something different" happened when Jonah sang and used the hand gestures to the song, "Jesus is the Rock of my Salvation." Following the singing, evidence of an untouched and unknown potential in Jonah's life was borne out when I read Psalm

23: Jonah recited the Psalm with me, using the King James Version! The young man whom others thought severely limited in his understanding of the world understood much more than the staff perceived. His recitation brought forth an audible silence on behalf of the staff present for the activity, while the kids just smiled and said, "Just listen to ol' Jonah!" and "That's it Jonah, keep talking!"

Jerry and Hal

The second case of suspicious signs of God's presence comes from another unit where a unique friendship has occurred. In spite of the individualistic culture of institutional life that tends to divide and separate people rather than bring people together, a budding friendship emerged between two young people. Jerry is the tall, handsome young African-American introduced in the chapter "Holy Surprises," who is here because of his violent, abusive nature. At first glance, he appears to be a hardcore, rugged individualist. His roommate is Hal, a young Native American who is usually gentle in his demeanor, though he is also known for losing control of his temper, and is labeled mentally retarded. These two young men, coming out of ethnic heritages that are considered "marginal" in American society, have struck up a remarkably close friendship. They go everywhere on the unit together, laughing together, admonishing one another, and enjoying their friendship, acting like natural brothers.

During the weekly time of "prayer and share" on the unit, Jerry has insisted that Hal come along with him for prayer. During this time of prayer and reflection upon the scriptures, the angry, abusive attitude of Jerry has never been seen, nor is the mercurial temperament of Hal present. Instead, the brotherhood between these two young men reveals a friendship of care and love that brings forth that which is good in both of them. Hal comes every week with Jerry to the "prayer and share." Jerry is teaching Hal the songs that we sing; Jerry is teaching him to read the Psalms with him, line by line; Jerry is reciting with him the Lord's Prayer, and is coaching Hal how to pray. If Hal ever gets agitated in the group, Jerry slows him down and explains what is happening. Jerry is his brother's keeper.

Jordie

The third case is about Jordie. Jordie, to quote his mother, has the body of a fifteen-year-old and a mind of a ten-year-old; Jordie is considered borderline mentally retarded. Recently, when Jordie and I were reading the story of Jesus walking on the water (Matthew 14:22–33), Jordie's eyes lit up, a big smile came upon his face, and he bellowed "I know a song that goes with that story!" With that, he began to sing a song about Jesus walking on the water, a capella. When I talked to his mother about Jordie's solo, she was amazed! She said they sang that song in a church they used to go to five years ago. Whenever there was time for the congregation to choose a song in worship, Jordie would always ask for that song. But he had not sung the song since they left the church.

These "cases" point to something strangely wonderful happening behind the walls of an institution that strives for strict control and predictability of all behavior. What is happening in the lives of these young people is something that can neither be controlled nor predicted by the practitioners of psychological (for example, behavioral psychology), or medical science. For when a company of people call upon the name of the Lord, and, in doing so, realize they are truly embedded in the presence of God's love, then a new, transforming order is revealed in the gathering of individuals who have become a community. This is the only explanation for what is happening in the lives of these young people who are considered by the professionals in the psychological and medical fields as disabled, limited in their ability to reason, let alone understand themselves, others, and God.

We know something that is considered "unusual" in the professional community is happening because of the physical evidence we are witness to—namely Jonah spontaneously recites a psalm, Jerry and Hal unexpectedly become friends, and Jordie sings. But where did Jonah first learn Psalm 23? Where did Jerry come to understand and practice the art of friendship? How has Jordie remembered his song? A partial theory or intuitive hunch: it most likely occurred somewhere around the church and the family in which they were raised and nurtured. Where else would they hear the scriptures read and reread? Where else would they learn about being one another's keeper? Where else could they learn their songs? It would not happen within a secular institution that, until recently, never had a chaplain, or in a culture that is highly suspicious of close friendships, and frowns upon unexpected noises among the children.

This hunch that something happened in and around a child's two primary communities of the church and the family reflects three important lessons. First, the importance of shaping and nurturing one another's Christian faith as an intentional, communal event, not as a spontaneous, individualistic, isolated, and occasional happening. Each one of us is born into our families and churches, taking in and discovering what it means to be part of a church and family through the sacred master stories being acted and sung out through the words spoken, the caring gestures performed, and the symbolic actions practiced in the rituals of the church and family.

Second, the words of the Apostle Paul seem to ring true in these stories, that neither "height nor depth, nor anything else in all creation will be able to separate us from the love of God in Christ Jesus our Lord" (Romans 8:39). Even behind the thick walls and double-locked doors of this secular institution, where the word of God was not to be spoken or shared until recently, memories of God's love, the songs sung, and the Psalms read in church still prevail and linger in the hearts and minds of the young people in the institution. Jonah's recitation of Psalm 23, and Jordie's unexpected memory of the song about Jesus walking on the water appears to confirm this hunch. As another young man shared with me, he feels sometimes like a hostage in this alien institution, removed from friends and family, that which is known and familiar. Even though many of the children did not regularly attend church when living at home, now, in this time of exile away from home, they think of God more often than ever before. In the times of prayer on the unit, many share their experiences of God's love, and they know that God's right hand shall hold them fast (Psalm 139:10).

Third concerns the observant eye, ear, nose, mouth, and sense of touch among all people, *including* those whom society has labeled "disabled." It appears that some people with disabling conditions, like Jonah and Jordie with mental retardation, and Jerry and Hal with behavioral and learning problems, have not been as unaware of what the rest of the world is doing as some professionals would have us believe. They have taken in all that their families and respective congregations have said and done with them, but have had no way or reason to communicate with others for no one bothered to ask them what they thought. When we find the pathway of communication that enables someone disabled to communicate with others, there is a sudden explosion of thoughts, feelings, and impressions shared by the ones we thought to be less than human.

What are the implications of these cases of people with "disabilities" for congregations and parishes? The largely nondisabled congregations, bold to claim that they are part of the body of Christ, need to under-stand that what they say and do, think and feel in the midst of their gathered assemblies, is being closely observed and monitored by those others whom society calls "disabled." The way that we care for one another, confront painful truths about our life together, the songs we sing, prayers we pray, pictures we draw, and the rituals we observe and participate in are all-powerful and potent rather than meek and ineffectual practices. These are all essential parts of learning, of faith being shaped and nurtured in the lives of all people, regardless of our seeming abilities or limitations; in the company of saints, both seen and unseen.

The proof that such learning happens in the church is found in the very material of these stories. It is in the church where Jerry learned to befriend others, in the company of his own church that he grew up in, where he was taught to be his brother's keeper. Jordie learned to sing of Jesus walking on the water. This is where Jonah learned Psalm 23 so well, able to recite it with others, acknowledging that "the Lord is my shepherd, I shall not want . . . surely goodness and mercy shall follow me all the days of my life, and I will dwell in the house of the Lord forever"—house that is open to everyone, regardless of abilities or limitations, at all times of our life.

20

The Importance of Stories in Acts of Caring

The novelist Barry Lopez writes that "everything is held together with stories. That is all that is holding us together, stories and compassion."[1] Narrative or story[2] does not only hold us together: narrative is equally crucial in understanding human life, for all that we are, and all that we do, and all that we think and feel is based upon stories, both our personal stories, and the stories of our significant community. The philosopher Richard Rorty claims that one of the most powerful ways of giving sense to one's life is by telling one's story amid a community. For by telling one's story we are able to fulfill our human desire for solidarity for and with other people.[3]

A glimpse of truth about the above statements has been revealed in the power of stories and storytelling witnessed by the writer in working with children and adolescents with severe behavioral or emotional disorders in a hospital setting. This first story focuses on the importance of our human stories in creating a community. The setting is a group therapy session that meets on a biweekly basis. Whenever a new adolescent or a new therapist comes into the group, there appears to be an unspoken ritual that is revealed in the group as a way of welcoming the new person to the group, and laying out the boundaries of the membership. One of the young people in the group takes the initiative and decides early on in a session that the new member in the group needs to be taught about the "history" of the group. This older member begins to tell the new member about some of the established members and rules of the group that are to be respected. In telling the new person these stories, others soon join in, filling in the blanks that the primary storyteller had forgotten or consciously left out of their rendition of the story.

This second story concerns the importance of the sacred, master stories of the religious community. During Passover I took two young men from the center to a seder meal on the first evening of Passover at a nearby temple. Throughout the service, I fought hard to remember the Hebrew alphabet, with consonants and vowels all mixed up, forgetting to read backward from right to left. The young men I brought to worship and the seder meal handled it far better than I did, following along with the service fairly well. We stayed for over three hours at the meal, until both of them looked quite tired, and one of the young men asked to go back to the hospital.

When I asked them about their experience of the evening, they told me that they had a good time: "It was nice to be among the majority tonight. They were reading [and acting out] a story that I've heard lots of times. This is *my* story." It was, indeed, their story that was being read and acted out, not fully my story. And those who are Jewish were in the majority, unlike the hospital where those who are Jewish are in the minority. For what makes one a Christian, a Jew, a Hindu, or a Muslim, is the sacred, master story of the religious community that shapes and nurtures each person's identity.

The third story is descriptive of the interaction of the human story in the context of the sacred story. Jordie, the young boy in this story, is borderline mentally retarded and has the body and the hormones of a boy who is fifteen-or sixteen-years-old.

Recently, the issue of masturbation came up as the young boy had been expressing some interest in sexual matters. But the mother was adamant with the hospital staff that as long as *her* pastor of *her* church disapproved of masturbation, her son would not be encouraged. To do so would be sinful. But after she talked to the pastor of her church, she gave her son permission to discuss sex with the hospital staff.

The final example has to do with the power of telling stories to a child, an act practiced in many homes and schools. The magically, engaging quality of stories is evident once a week in the religious story time on the hospital's unit for young children, ages seven to twelve, many of whom are labeled Attention Deficit/Hyperactive Disorder. In other words, many of these young children are hyperactive, each individual child struggling hard not to provoke another child or staff member. Yet once a week, six to twelve individual children literally stop bouncing off of each other and gather together and sit quietly for fifteen minutes, creating and sharing a common space while engaged in a common task: attentively listening to the stories from both the Bible and Dr. Seuss or an Ananzi tale from Africa. They are quiet, with their eyes fixed on the pages of the book, captured by the story being spun by the reader.

The Basic Importance of Stories

What all these examples reveal is the power of hearing, sharing, and telling stories in the many acts of caring for young children with behavior disorders in a hospital setting. The reason that there is such power in storytelling is because life is best understood and has meaning when we consider it as an ongoing story. In truth, there is no way to live life without story.

Relating to one another, as one story among many others, is natural to all human beings. Story itself is a natural gift, shared among all in the human race. The natural scientist Daniel Dennett argues that while it is natural for spiders to weave webs, and beavers to build dams, none of them with any degrees in either art or architecture, it is also natural for human beings to tell and listen—or better yet *to communicate* with one another—through stories.[4] The psychologist Jerome Bruner echoes this sentiment, stating that what we all share in common, regardless of our abilities or limitations, is that we are creatures of story and history.[5] History, itself, is biography writ large. For each person and the community one is part of, is a story unto themselves, with a beginning, a middle, and an end, set in a certain time and space, in a concrete place.[6]

Story or narrative may also serve as an epistemological lens: "How do we know what we know?" Our knowledge of ourselves, others in our human communities, and the world in general is continually shaped and nurtured by the stories that we tell and listen to throughout life in the various communities of people that we live with. For example, the new member of the group therapy session is welcomed by receiving the story of the group as well as much gossip. The young men are proud of their Jewish community's story told in the midst of Passover. By participating in the story of Passover, they are reaffirmed in their identity as children of Abraham. And the anxious mother is quieted about her fears and questions of her adolescent son's budding sexuality by listening to others who share her belief in the truthfulness of the Christian story.

Besides shaping one's identity, the telling of stories, itself, may physically shape and nurture the human brain. Joseph Chilton Pearce, a former professor of the humanities, wrote that in storytelling there is the stimulus of words, which brings about the production of inner images, an extraordinary creative play involving the brain:

> Each new story requires a whole new set of neural connections and reorganization of visual activity within a major challenge for the brain. Television, by providing all that action synthetically, is handled by the same, limited number of neural structures regardless of programming, since the brain's work has already been done for it. So neural potential goes unrealized and development is impaired— unless storytelling and play are provided as well as television, or preferably, instead of television.[7]

It is in the moments of the religious story time with the young children that one can almost see the ideas and images painted in the context of the book percolate within these young, engaged minds.

In this narrative worldview, a child is more than a body of data, facts and figures, a composite of behaviors that can be predicted and controlled. This narrative approach assumes that a child is a living, breathing, changing person, sometimes in control of some of the events in life, and at other times controlled by these same events. What makes the narrative interesting is that, as it is being lived out, it is by and large unpredictable in nature. All that one can predict, if there is still the need to predict someone else's action, is that all people are, by and large, unpredictable. What holds each person together is not only one's individual story, but the actual community stories that one shares in common with others.[8]

What keeps each individual's story together, providing the unity and sense of purpose in each person's life, is the master story that we are embedded in, surrounded by, and guided by, told and retold by the community of meaning in which we are integral members. Religious communities are, themselves, the primary communities of meaning for many, entrusted with sharing and retelling the master, often sacred, story. During holidays, people in families regale each other with what happened to whom on a certain holiday of the years. In the religious communities, the master story is ascribed as also being sacred. Examples of such sacred stories include the Hebrew Bible, the Quran, and the Old and New Testaments of the Christian faith, all of which hold in their pages the story of a people gathered together, living out their belief and relationship with God in this world.

With a basic understanding of the centrality of narrative in human life, as shown in the above examples, the telling and listening of stories plays an essential part in any act of caring in human communities, especially in caring for young children with behavior disorders and emotional problems. In the following section, there will be an exploration of the importance of stories in the various health provider service fields, including medicine, psychotherapy, education, and pastoral care. In one sense, what all these diverse fields share in common, rooted in very different paradigms, is story.

The Place of Stories in the Caring Professions

Narrative, writes the philosopher Paul Ricoeur, is built upon concern for the human condition: stories reach sad, comic, or absurd denouements, while theoretical ideas reach conclusive or inconclusive arguments.[9] Theology and literature do not have the market on stories. All professional health service providers, who work with children with severe emotional and behavioral disorders—like pastoral counselors, psychologists, social workers, and nurses—are concerned about the human condition, and are intimately involved in the act of restorative health care. In light of the above examples, caring for others with emotional or behavioral disorders allows all professionals the opportunity to see the beauty and brutality of the human condition. The professionals involved in this work are continually amazed at what these young people will do in life, for whenever the professional thinks of the worst thing that the children could do, the children never do it. They do something else that the professional never thought or dreamt possible.

The role and function of narrative, as an integral part in the many acts of caring, is centrally important and makes itself known in various fields in the following areas:

Therapy and Stories

1. *Seeing One Another as a Storyteller.* In entering into a therapeutic relationship with another person, like a child with emotional problems, it is important to remember that each one of us comes into the world with the ability and desire to express and receive stories. Our first days of life after birth are spent becoming part of the story of our families and a larger community of meaning, for we are born story listeners, taking in the stories of the immediate and extended family. For example, in many families with young children, there are various moments in life when a child wishes to be told a story about when the mother or father were little children, with the child eagerly awaiting to hear the details of growing up.

Therapeutically, psychologists have been arguing that the self, or ego, is the primary storyteller. The ego is cast in the role of a storyteller, continually constructing narratives about life. Self, writes the psychologist Jerome Bruner, is not a static thing or substance, but a configuring (and reconfiguring) of personal events into an historical unity, which is not only what has been done, but what is happening, and what is anticipated to happen.[10]

The psychologist George Howard argues that the development of identity is the construction of a life story. Psychopathology is an instance of life stories gone awry, and psychotherapy serves as exercises in the repair of stories that are broken.[11] In some ways, the therapist has a chance to help the individual child or family to understand that they each have an important story to share with others. They also have an active part in composing their own story, and more importantly, contribute in helping others in the act of writing their story of life.

2. *We Are a Story That Tells Itself in Time.* While some therapists may take the above constructivist approach that assumes one constructs one's own life story, others argue that, for the most part, we neither spin nor compose our own stories: stories that we inherit or are born into spin us. Therefore, our human consciousness, our narrative selves, are a product and *not* the source of the story we are living out. In other words, each person inherits much of the story that one lives and tells others.[12]

This understanding of a story's powerful influence over others is reinforced among many professionals who work with families who point out that such social taboos as incest, physical abuse, and alcoholism in the family is often a story, or a script of life, that is learned and passed on and sadly repeated from one generation to the next. The psychoanalyst Alice Miller writes that many of the problems and traumas that some adults face in life are caused during their childhood by a parent who may have felt insecure and seen the child as a preferred sexual object.[13] In order to change the story told and lived out of abuse and neglect, there needs to be the identification of the center of the narrative gravity, which is in control of the narrative-spinning human body.

Education and Stories

The educator Kieran Egan believes that stories shape a child's understanding of the world around them. Story, itself, is linked to our imaginations, our ability to form mental images of what is not actually present or has never been actually experienced. With such power in stories, it is important not to treat stories in a willy-nilly fashion. Instead, it makes sense to use the natural power of stories to communicate with children more effectively.[14]

Stories are clearly effective in telling people about some of the practical skills of daily life, as well as some of the moral truths of life. Good and bad, right and wrong, are concepts best described and understood in the telling of stories—for example, in a romantic fairy tale like *Beauty and the Beast*, or in the radical autobiography of *Malcolm X*. In the example of religious story time, the act of telling stories whether from the Bible or Dr. Seuss even engages the scattered attention of the young children with behavior disorders.

However, stories not only educate us about others; they are also educational in revealing knowledge about ourselves, which is an invaluable lesson as a child grows into adulthood in the following ways.

1. *Stories Tell Us Who We Are.* The story that we are part of and inherit shapes *who* we are. Our parents, brothers, sisters, aunts, uncles, grandparents, cousins, and the extended community, and the bits and pieces of the story that each one has for us and us for them, is an essential in the educational task of shaping and nurturing our very character. *Who* we are will help decide *what* we will do, and *how* we do what we do in this world.

2. *Stories Tell Us Whose We Are.* The master, sacred story that we are born into also marks us in another fundamental way: being born into a family, we are also part of something that began before we were born, an identity that we inherit and that marks us for life. In other

words, *who* we are is preceded by the claim of *whose* we are. In a broader sense, we are shaped, cultural anthropologists argue, by the myths and sacred stories of religious communities which each culture transmits to its new members. Such stories play an important role in shaping our minds, our values, our understanding and appreciation of life itself.

For example, consider the above story of the adolescents at the hospital and their visit to a synagogue on the first night of Passover. While living in the hospital, they are exposed to many of the Christian holidays and celebrations. They both felt wonderfully refreshed after going to the synagogue. The refreshment was not only from gathering together with other people who were Jewish; they had a new appreciation for both listening to and reciting in a congregation of other people who were Jewish *their* story of the Passover. The young adolescents could truly appreciate the Passover story unlike many others attending the ritualistic dinner, because these young people had been living in an "alien land," where their story, their identity of who and whose they are, is rarely told.

Theology and Stories.

The theologian James McClendon wrote that "every theology is linked to some narratives; successful theology, knowing this, discovers and renovates its own narrative base."[15] Our very understanding of God and life is dependent upon some reference to a story of someone's experience of God; some plot and character in some setting, which is the stuff of stories.

To tell or to hear a story is, itself, a moral act for the following reasons.

1. *To Tell a Story Is a Moral Act.* In telling and listening to stories, no longer are right and wrong, good and bad, love and hate, trust and mistrust, hope and despair, care and inhospitality, abstract concepts. These abstract concepts, which lose much in theoretical discussions, now become known and real because they are embedded in human stories. For example, the theologian Stanley Hauerwas argues that "care," by itself, outside the context of story, is ambiguous. Care is a context-dependent term, whose meaning is indefinite until specified within a particular context, often provided by principles, roles, and institutions.[16]

Another example is the word "community." It is impossible to describe community without having a story to place it in, or to experience it from. For example, consider this Midrashic story of community, told by Elie Wiesel:

> A man is on a boat. He is not alone but acts as if he were. One night, he begins to cut a hole under his seat. His neighbors shriek: "Have you gone mad? Do you want to sink us all?" Calmly he answers them: "I don't understand what you want. What I'm doing is none of your business. I paid my way. I'm only cutting under my own seat."[17]

In an interesting twist on individualism versus community responsibility, the reader and hearer draws from the story the understanding that community means caring enough to pay attention to what one does in the rowboat of life, for it will have a direct influence upon the fate and hope of others in the rowboat.

2. *To Forget the Story Is a Grievous Act.* Forgetting the narratives of self, family, and community is inhuman, because our human accumulated suffering and happiness is then gone and forgotten. For example, we have a photo album in our family that has no names written on any of the pictures. Just black and white photos with figures in beautiful long dresses and handsome formal coats and ties from the early 1900s. Their story is no longer told, and any idea of who they are was lost with the death of grandparents and other relatives.

The theologian Johann Baptist Metz wrote that traditions, rituals, and stories of community life need to be remembered, for once they have been extinguished, then inhumanity begins.[18] This same thought is eloquently expressed by the writer Elie Wiesel, who has often said that once the stories of the Holocaust are forgotten and silenced, then Hitler, and any other despotic ruler, will have won.

Some Implications of Stories in Acts of Caring

Knowing that stories influence virtually every aspect of human life, it is important to understand how a narrative approach to religious education, pastoral counseling in particular, and health care in general, influence the act of caring. To begin with, the narrative approach directly influences how we interact with others. Seeing each person as an ongoing story is a perspective shared by the physician and poet

William Carlos Williams, who saw his sick patients who were young children as a story being lived out and wanting to be told and to be heard. Treating the child without listening and knowing essential parts of the life story is treating the condition and not the whole child.[19]

The medical ethicist Daniel Callahan writes that professionals in fields like medicine, social work, psychology, and education, must understand that there is a biographical vantage point that we need to consider in working with a person who has a disability.[20]

Arthur Kleinman, who wrote *The Illness Narratives*,[21] said that to fully appreciate the sick person's and family's experiences, the clinician must first piece together the illness narrative as it emerges from the patient's complaints and explanatory model, because patients order their experiences of illness as personal narrative. That is how patients understand what they are experiencing in life. Life is narrative-based.

There is also healing in the sharing of stories with others. In the act of caring, the care-giver is also a self, a subject, not an object, free-floating, unattached to others. As care-givers, our ego is also cast in the role of storyteller and story-listeners, as we tell and listen to the stories that the patient, client, or child is revealing to us.

The educational ethnographer Richard Katz, in exploring healing and transformation in the Fiji and Kung cultures, noticed that in the act of healing, the healer, in the midst of the ritual celebration that would ultimately heal another person, would have to give something of him or herself in order for the other person to be healed.[22] There is a relationship, a sharing of stories that goes on in the units of a hospital, as doctors, nurses, family therapists, social workers, teachers, maintenance folks, and pastors share life with disabled children and adolescents. Some are calling this participatory learning and caring; others see it as relational learning and caring.

What is also important is how aware each one of us, individually, is of our *own* life story, and how our individual narrative influences and shapes our worldview, our understanding of the human condition. We have to hear, interpret, and respond to the narratives of others, both among those we work with as well as those in our care.

Finally, there is a reservoir of healing power in telling the truths of the sacred story of a religious community. Again, the writer Barry Lopez writes that the power of the master, sacred story—stories that we inherit or embed ourselves in—is the power to reorder a state of psychological confusion through contact with the pervasive truth found in the context of the master, sacred story. The power of the narrative is to nurture and heal, to repair a spirit in disarray.[23]

The true role of the storyteller-as-care-worker is to bring about a chance to guide the child or adolescent to listen to the truth of the master, sacred story that they have inherited from their community of meaning, be it family-bound or religious community like a church or synagogue. In working with young people with emotional problems, it is an invaluable way of helping the young person to identify a master, sacred story that gives them life and truth, and not more lies. For lying is the opposite of story.

In conclusion, stories are invaluable in all caring professions that work with disabled children and adolescents. By sharing our stories together, our attention is focused and a common space is created in which young people can truly discover the meaning behind many of life's episodes. Listening and receiving the stories of the religious community, placing one's life story in the larger context of the religious community's sacred story, enables a young person to understand who they are, because they now know whose they are. Listening to the sacred story of the religious community provides the necessary guidance in making it through what often appears to be amoral, ambiguous dilemmas of our age.

In the act of telling and listening, expressing and receiving the stories of life with one another, care becomes real, for we only share stories with those whom we care for and about. People instinctively know that they are cared for and able to therefore care for others when someone takes the other person's story seriously. Through the story, in the midst of this caring act, true healing of head and heart occurs. People are able to move on in their journey of faith and life with the support of others and their stories. And the story as an act of care becomes a true sign of love.

• • •

In the next three chapters, there are examples of the power of God's sacred story as collected and recorded in the Bible, in shaping and nurturing the Christian faith of three young men. Each adolescent comes from a different family background and experiences in their respective churches. Nonetheless, all three consider themselves Christian. Their stories reflect the power of God's sacred story to spin our human stories and directly shape our faith.

21

Listen, Real Hard this Time, to the Gospel of God

Fred Craddock, a professor of preaching at Candler School of Theology, believes that what often happens to Christians is that they listen, again and again, to so many of the Bible stories without being challenged in *how* to be a Christian that they soon become numb to the power of the message inherent in God's story.[1] As a result of this spiritual numbing, many Christians merely turn off and do not tune in to the stories of God's miraculous acts of love and compassion, justice and truth. However, when people no longer listen or hear both the letter and the spirit of the message about God's love for this world, people begin to forget whose they are, unable to figure out where they belong in the body of Christ.

When Christians no longer hear and therefore understand the challenging yet encouraging words found in scriptures and articulated in the community of Christ, the journey of faith becomes directionless. The people of God begin to lose a vision of the quest they are on in this life. The temptation to wander from the Christian journey of faith is already strong enough; to quote the Christian hymn, "Come Thou Fount of Every Blessing," "prone to wander Lord I feel it, prone to leave the God I love."

One of the corrective ways of dealing with this urge to wander from God is in living, working, learning, and worshiping with people whom society has decided have some disabilities. By no means are the children and adolescents I have worked with "divine interpreters of the word of God" because of a sense of "holy innocence." Instead, many of these children and adolescents have never been included in the numerous readings and rereadings, tellings and retellings of the gospel stories as told in Sunday schools, youth programs, or in their respective congregations or parishes. When they come upon some passages in the Bible, they come with such wonder, awe, and deep reverence for what they are hearing for the first time. They believe that these are the very words of God in Christ. Those of us who have heard it before may share, again, in the contagious exuberance that these young people are experiencing in receiving the good news. Many act as if they are tasting sweet honey, relishing the sweetness in their mouths.

One of the young people who displayed such exuberance for God's story was Jordie. I met Jordie on his *second* admission to the hospital. As was mentioned in the previous two chapters, Jordie has, in the words of his mother, "the body of a fifteen-year-old teenager, and the mind of a ten year old boy." In other words, he is slightly developmentally delayed, and has had some problems negotiating the social mores of either a fifteen- or ten-year-old child. He looks to be growing to six feet tall, thin as a rail, friendly and shy to a fault.

Jordie is Joanne's only child from a now-separated marriage. Jordie has a history of going around the neighborhood they were living in, and inviting himself into homes when no one was at home, as well as staying too long for "visits" and not leaving when asked to leave. Many mothers and fathers would not let their young children play with Jordie, because he had the body of an older young man though the mind of a young boy. They were fearful of what he might do with their children sexually. According to Joanne, he has been known to "swear a blue streak in church and Sunday school." However, Jordie is also gullible, and has often borne the brunt of the practical jokes that other children have instigated in school.

When he had first arrived at the hospital, six months earlier, Joanne was shocked that there was no one at the facility who would take care of, let alone address her child's, spiritual needs, or, for that matter, her spiritual needs and concerns. She felt very guilty about having her son admitted to a psychiatric facility, but she could do no more with him at home. Even though he had been admitted for short-term hospitalization during one summer, that respite was not enough. Life with Jordie was too chaotic and out of her control for him to live in the home or neighborhood anymore.

In hopes of finding some guidance from God, to whom she had cried her pleas for help more than once (she assured me) as to where she should take her son for help, she went to her church. She asked the pastor for some guidance in this delicate area, for no one she knew had ever had one of their children admitted to a psychiatric facility.

But the pastor was of little to no help. At first, the pastor politely listened to her as she explained what had been happening with her son at home and in the neighborhood. When she asked the pastor for some names of pastoral counselors or Christian psychiatrists, some references as to where to take her son for help, he said, "Let me think about that, and I'll get back to you in the coming week." Unfortunately, this became the same, tired response each Sunday she went to him after the worship service for help and guidance. The pastor shook her hands, appeared to listen as he guided her through the line of other parishioners waiting to talk and greet their pastor. No longer does Joanne attend that church, but she continues to hold onto her deep-seated anger towards the pastor.

After meeting Joanne and Jordie, Joanne soon left for home in Georgia, leaving Jordie at the hospital. When I first met Jordie on the hospital unit, he was very excited about the opportunity to talk about God, Jesus, the Holy Spirit, and church. He drew me a picture of his church, drawing in an organ because "I love to sing songs to Jesus like [now actually singing the song] 'And he walks with me and he talks with me, and he tells me I am his own!'"

Then I asked him what his favorite Bible verse was: "It has got to be 'The Lord is my shepherd, I shall not want, He makes me lie down in green pastures.'" I pulled out a children's Bible, *Tomie DePaola's Book of Bible Stories*,[2] filled with bright, colorful pictures that capture the essence of the story. I asked him if he would like to meet weekly and talk about these stories. Jordie's shy grin unfolded into a broad smile, with a "You bet, Dr. Brett [my title at the hospital]. That would be great!"

With Jordie's interest in the Bible, and love for listening and talking about the stories of God's presence in human history, we began to meet on a regular, weekly basis, discussing either verses from the Bible that he remembers, or stories randomly chosen from the book of *Bible Stories* by Tomie DePaola. This first time we got together to talk about the stories from the Bible occurred after one of his first days at his new school on campus. He had been teased in school, and he remembered a verse from Psalm 23 that I had told him a week earlier: "The Lord is my shepherd, I shall not want":

> I know He's with me. Lately, I been . . . now when I get upset at school or something, I pray to Jesus, and I ask him to help me. I been doing that lately, and He's been helping me. The Lord has been helping me make it through school for the rest of the day.
>
> When I get upset, sometimes I don't always pray to the Lord. I get mad and cuss or something, instead of praying to the Lord. But lately, instead of getting upset, I just pray to the Lord and ask Him to help me not to do those things and stuff.

One way that he is able to deal with his anger is to remember the good times that he had in church, like when he is singing his favorite song, "'I Love to Praise His Name,' I felt like I wanted to sing it and I went out in front of the church after we were singing in the choir, so I did that and I felt good about it." In this session, Jordie said what made him happiest in the world right now was to "be able to serve Jesus." When I asked him if he could serve Jesus here at the hospital, Jordie looked right in my eyes and said, "Yeah, you can serve God all the time."

The next time we met, Jordie had just been to a showing of the Walt Disney movie *Beauty and the Beast* with other young people from his unit. Filled with fantastical thoughts, Jordie was ready to choose a miracle story from among the Bible story book—Jesus walking on the water:

> That's the start of a song! Can I sing a song to you now? We used to sing this song at our church . . . "Jesus walks on the water . . . I feel the wings of mercy" . . . I'm thinking of this song that we sing . . . "there ain't no power of hell gonna stop God's wings of love" . . . we sing that at the church of God where we go.

I asked Jordie if he can walk on the water: "Yeah, I reckon." I asked him if he really could walk on the water without sinking, and on second thought he said "Nah." Who is it who can? "Jesus, because he can do everything."

Jesus Walks on the Water (Matt. 14:22–33)

A week later we come together in my office, and he began by wanting to draw for me a picture of Jesus, "because I want to talk about Jesus today." After talking about school, his speech therapy session, and one of his favorite subjects, art, I gave him the Bible story book, and Jordie chose to read the story of "Jesus Feeds the five thousand." I asked him what Jesus did in this story, only able to get a few words in edgewise through the entire discussion of this story:

> [Jesus blessed the bread and broke it] and he said that when they have leftovers, Jesus was able to get like all those people who didn't have food . . . a way for them to get food. Jesus was able to provide food, for they was in need, like when you in need, like when you don't feel good or you need food or something, Jesus will always be there to help you feel better or get you food and stuff. He's always there to bless people.

Why?

> Because he cares about people on earth, and He don't want them to be poor and go hungry. He cares about us.

How much?

> A lot . . . When you in need or something, Jesus is there to offer you food, or provide you, to feel better if you sick or something and you pray to God about it he'll hear you and you'll feel better and he'll bless you.

Is that what God means by good news?

> Yes . . . because if you felt bad or something I could pray for you and if I felt bad and I asked you to pray for me you could pray for me? And I'd feel better?

Does God have more power than a therapist?

> Yeah, because if you felt bad I could pray for you or I could come to you and ask you to pray for me.

That would be nice.

Yeah.

God Creates the World (Gen. 1)

At this point in our relationship, Jordie is very excited about getting together and reading the Bible stories. We read the Bible account of creation (Genesis 1), "In the beginning God created . . .

> the heavens and the earth. And God said let there be light, and there will be light . . . [Jordie continues to read the entire story]. This is a long story! It says that God created us in his image, which is true.

I asked Jordie to go ahead and draw his picture of creation and what it would look like, from his own, contemporary, Floridalike perspective:

> Maybe the clouds, the sky and the sun. Then on the second day, God created the grass. And after the grass, God created plants . . . yeah, God made plants. Then on the next day, God made a tree. God only made one tree. Then on the third day, the sea. Can I draw a sidewalk? God created the sidewalk, or it wouldn't be here, and the parking lot. Amen. That's the sidewalk. After that, he created the stars, that go out at night time. Let's see here, he created the parking lot. That's a car. And then God made this building, or this building wouldn't be here in Melbourne, wouldn't have nowhere to go, be outside all our life. God created the building and he created two doors.

And what did God say at the end of all this creation?

Done!

Did you draw everything you wanted in this picture?

I reckon I drew everything. Amen.

Jesus Enters Jerusalem (Mark 10, 11)

The next session we had was near Palm Sunday. So I began this time with Jordie's talking about Jesus riding into Jerusalem on the back of a donkey. Jordie remembers most of the Bible stories since he grew up in a church, and he remembered this story as well as he did the other stories:

> I like the part where it says, "Blessed is He who comes in the name of the Lord." That means if the poor needed something to eat, Jesus would come in the name of the Lord and be able to give them food.

I asked him to describe the scene if he were in Jerusalem when Jesus came riding through town on the donkey:

> I'd give Jesus some money . . . to help the poor folks, heal them. If they wasn't saved, God could reach out and touch them and heal them.

Do you like this parade?

> Yeah. You could pray with Jesus, and maybe he'd reach out [to you]. If you prayed with Jesus, he would reach out. You could give him money to help the poor folks or God could reach out to heal them, and praying with Jesus.

Do you remember what happens around Easter?

> When they nailed [him], and he bled and stuff, he did that kind of for us, right? He died so that when he came back, we could be born again? Right.

Love is Most Important (1 Cor. 13)

After Easter, I let Jordie pick out the next Bible story, and he chose the reading from 1 Corinthians. And so we read together about Christian love, according to the Apostle Paul. I asked Jordie what is love after reading that passage aloud:

> It means love is patient and is kind. It means Jesus loves us. Like when we go to church and clap and sing and praise God, he does it cause he'd rather us praise him than the devil. I know that's for sure. [Love is] praising God. You love your parents and appreciate what they do for you [because you love them].

What does it mean to be kind?

> It means Jesus is kind to us; he loves us. [Being kind to someone means] speaking to you, like "Hey, good morning, how you doin' today?" Like every morning, like this morning, and the past mornings when I go up to the switchboard, like in the morning when they be working, I be saying "Good Morning, Switchboard!"

Where does love begin?

> Jesus. You can have love at school or work. I can have love, like here at the hospital, and pray and stuff to the Lord, because he's always with you. Just like when we go to church, my Mamma said that the Lord's not just with you in church, she was explaining to me one time, and she was telling me how the Lord is always with you.

So, faith, hope and love, but the greatest of these is which?

> Jesus.

The Lord Watches over You (Psalm 121:1–8)

Jordie began this session, reading parts of Psalm 121: "I lift up my eyes to the hills—where does my help come from? My help comes from the Lord, the maker of heaven and earth." He reads the passage aloud, tripping over some words, but not too many. He has heard the Psalm read before in church, and "it is a favorite of mine," he tells me. I ask him, "What does this Psalm mean for you?"

> It means that no matter where you are at and you need to pray or something, God's always with you; He's right there, there and then. Everywhere.

Is that Good News?

> Yes . . . because he's always with us.

So I lift up my eyes to the hills.

> Where does my help come? My help comes from the Lord, because when we need him, he's there for us.

And who is God?

He will not let your . . .

No, who is God? The creator of . . .

Heaven.

And . . .

Earth.

He will not let your foot . . .

slip, no he won't. He watches over Israel and neither slumbers nor sleeps.

So what does this all mean?

God's watchin' over us . . . all the time . . . the Lord watches over you. The Lord God is your shade at your right.

What does it mean when it says that the Lord will keep you from all harm?

It means that He will keep us from all, like when we in trouble and we go to pray, he'll keep us from harm. He's right there . . . he'll pray with us.

Does God like to pray with us?

Yeah. The Lord will watch over your coming and going, both now and forever more.

So wherever you walk, or wherever you are . . .

Wherever you at, God's with you, twenty-four hours, day and night!

Can you ever leave God?

> No. He wouldn't be pleased at all.

Is God ever going to leave you?

> No, even if you leave God, you ain't got nothing to worry about, God's still with you . . . even if you don't like God, that mean God still loves you and he cares about your life.

It's an amazing love.

> That's why it says, "and let everything praise the Lord."

Praise the Lord Everywhere (Psalm 148: 1–14)
This was our last meeting, and Jordie chose this Psalm for this time of leavetaking: "Praise the Lord. Praise the Lord from the heavens, praise him in the heights above. Praise him, all his angels, praise him, all his heavenly hosts."
It has been drilled into Jordie that one way to praise the Lord is by praying to God. And so we ended this time together talking about the power of prayer:

> Like my grandma . . . we keep praying for her, that she . . . she used to go to church, like every Sunday, and she wouldn't go a lot, and now she's going every Sunday, with [one of my Aunts].

So the miracle was . . .

> We kept praying for that miracle to happen, so it finally happened.

Prayer is powerful in our lives:

> When I pray to Him, I feel better and stuff, like at home. When we was at home, one night, right before we go to bed, my mamma always tells me to kneel down on the floor and we'll pray. One night, she was tired, and she said we wasn't going to pray. I said, "No, that's not right. Even if you tired, we supposed to pray." So she got on the floor with me and we prayed.

Do you want to pray now?

You can.

And with that, I prayed for both of us, and that God would help us to remember these times together throughout our lives. Amen.

• • •

Jordie left for another facility, what is considered a "step down" facility, where there are not many doors locking him up. His mother was glad that he left this place with a bit more respect for himself and for others, and that he seemed to learn something about boundaries, respecting the space each person needs in his or her life, including his own. What saddened her was that there was no further opportunity for him to go to church in the new facility, and no one there to talk about God, a "topic" that Jordie enjoyed talking about.

The one theme that kept on coming out of all our conversations together is that God is everywhere, and knows where we are at all times. This was reassuring news for him, and for us. Nothing can separate us from the love of God: "neither death, nor life, nor angels, nor rulers, nor things present, nor things to come, nor powers, nor height, nor depth, nor anything else in all creation, will be able to separate us from the love of God in Christ Jesus our Lord" (Rom. 8:38–39). These are more than reassuring words for Jordie: this is a truth that he clings to as a child clings to a parent for caring support in times of travail. Being hundreds of miles away from his home and family, he tenaciously holds onto God's words, God's promises, as shared among Christians who are far from the church family he has worshiped with all these years. Why does Jordie hold onto God? "Because I am close to God's heart. I know I am."

22

Steve and the Behavior Mod God

At the hospital, a quick way to get my attention is for a child, and sometimes a staff member, to say that they do not believe in God anymore. Automatically, without thinking about who said it or why they said it, I will ask: "What have you done that you don't think God loves you?" Often the response is that the person has prayed and prayed to God about something on their mind, inquired and asked God for guidance, help, or material sustenance, and still God does not come through quick enough with the desired response of the petitioner. Petitioners further explain that they have done all that they thought they had to do, and then go through a mental, or sometimes written, check list of their "dos and don'ts" in my presence: "I've prayed and prayed, worked through the rosary, and prayed again, that I would go home, or that my Dad would die, or my mother would visit me, or my social worker would get me out of here . . . and none of those things has happened yet. I've worked and done all the good things that I'm supposed to do, but God just doesn't seem to hear my prayer, because none of my requests has come true."

For an example of this theological approach to God and answered prayer, consider June, who is convinced that the number of times one prays is going to bring God around to do her bidding. Thirteen-year-old June has been sexually abused by a member of her family, and one of the ways that she knows how to get attention is by offering sexual favors to others. Almost every time that I come onto the unit floor, June is one of the first in line to ask for me to pray her prayer request for her, warning me to "be sure when you pray tonight that you pray that my dad is released from prison and that I can go home soon after he and my mom go for family therapy, OK? Be sure you've got that and you pray that when you go to bed tonight, OK? Be sure you pray that, got that?"

Even though I may suggest that we must have faith that God hears our prayers the first time we pray, June is nevertheless adamant and insistent that I pray for her. Daily. If not hourly. Every day she makes this request of me, because she believes that the more times you actually, physically pray, the better the chance that God has heard and will answer the prayer positively. By praying a certain number of times, one can predict and control God's power to answer prayers.

When I asked June and the other children how they know that God has not heard their prayer, they say that if God *had* heard their prayer, then their requests and suggestions would have been answered by God in a satisfactory and quick order. Therefore, since their request has not come to pass after a specific period of time set by the child, if their question has not been satisfactorily answered, then they do not believe in God anymore, and they do not think that they need God, because God does not seem to need or want them. One young person left such a discussion with me about God's inability to answer her prayers, saying smugly: "Take that, Spiritual Dude and your God," as if she had shot me in the spirit with a gun. She did not walk away with a smile on her face, but dejectedly, afraid that God was deadened to her requests, as well as to the requests other human beings make. To these children, God appeared to be ignoring their plaintive cries.

What kind of image do these young people have of God? This insipid, distorted, crooked image of God is the "Behavior Mod God." These young people construct and sustain this image of such an angry, controlling God as a direct result of the intensive overwhelming behavior modification or behavior analysis programs in the institution. The young people with emotional, behavioral, or developmental disabilities order their lives according to the behavioral program that undergirds their extended treatment in a residential treatment program or psychiatric facility.

These behavioral programs are based upon the science of behaviorism, which is the belief that human behavior can be conditioned, predicted, and controlled, for we are but a complex machine or simple animal. Introspection of any kind or felt sensations are not observable, and therefore are not important. Men and women, like preprogrammed machines or simple animals, respond to certain kinds of external stimuli that have the power to control and shape our lives. All that matters or counts in life is our overt behavior. No longer are we concerned about what is on a person's mind or, metaphorically speaking the heart, because all introspective, reflective terms are counted as insignificant and thus eliminated from the vocabulary of some psychologists and educators.

Theologically speaking, behaviorism is based upon an ethic of works . . . good works versus bad works, to be more exact. Simplistically speaking, the good works are rewarded and reinforced, while the bad or "negative works" are to be "extinguished." The Behavior Mod God rewards and reinforces our good, overt behaviors and observable acts of goodwill, with the likely chance that the people who rack up the most number of "good acts" will go to heaven. Meanwhile, God will be punishing those of us for the negative or inappropriate behaviors, with hell as the ultimate time-out room. Salvation depends on what one *does* with one's individual life. There is no room in this simplistic, cosmological worldview for grace or atonement: salvation and justification depend solely upon the works of the lonely, individualistic, isolated "you" and "me".

Living life by such a theological worldview is captured in the life story shared with me by Steve. Steve is a fifteen-year-old, over six feet tall, has blonde hair and blue eyes. His haircut is unique for he has a crew cut around his head, except for the very front, on which there is a thatch of long blonde hair hanging in his eyes. He has three earrings in his left ear, and he wears T-shirts, usually tie-dyed T-shirts, with various slogans and messages printed on them. Some thought that he was a punk rocker when he came into the hospital . . . until he shared his likes and dislikes in music as a fan of the Motown sound.

Steve is also a Christian, having been baptized while he was at a camp for adolescent males with behavior disabilities, Bethany Academy of Christian Living:

> I learned I could do all things through Christ that strengthen me.
> I learned to be my own leader with Christ and not a follower of
> Satan. The discipline was basically writing extra Bible verses at
> night and memorize Bible verses. It was basically a real nice place.
> A ranch on fifty-seven acres.

He wound up at the Academy after living in other institutions for children with behavioral and emotional disabilities, starting when he was only nine years old. He said that his problems started at school, when other children would pick on him because he was smaller and he would not fight back: "Then one day I started to fight back and I would get in trouble and they wouldn't." His mother took him to a psychologist, who thought it would be good for Steve to attend a nearby institution for children with behavior problems.

However, Steve did not only have trouble with other school children: Steve also assaulted his mother, which landed him in six or seven hospitals and institutions for short and long periods of times. He has been in crisis units as well as in acute care hospitals. The longest period of time that he has lived with his grandmother, mother, step-brother, and step-sister is three months in the last seven years. After three months, something always goes wrong, and Steve ends up back in an institution. At one point in our many conversations, Steve was so exasperated with his family that he plaintively cried out: "What's a matter with them? Can't they understand I don't like them and don't want to live with them? I burned down their house, ruin their animals, yell at them all the time . . . can't they get it through their heads that I don't want to live with them?"

For Steve, home is not where his heart is. His biological mother gave him up for adoption to his grandmother. He calls his biological mother his "sister," and his grandmother his "mother." He has no ideas as to the whereabouts of his father. His biological mother had two other children whom Steve "kind of likes." He has an uncle in the north, but has no other relative that he knows of at this time. While his "mother" admits to being a Christian, Steve has judged that no one in the family, save himself, is a Christian.

Life has not been easy for Steve. Though he does not believe in Satan, he admits to doing the things that Satan would do, like "assault and battery, stealing, breaking and entering, setting houses on fire," and assorted acts of vandalism and mischief of one kind or another. Steve set his "mother's" house on fire, as well as admitted to hurting some of her animals. He admits that he probably has some behavioral problems. He says that these problems are not of his own making, but due to a chemical imbalance in his body.

Even with this background, Steve believes in God. To Steve, God is omnipotent:

I understand Him to be the most powerful. No one can be better, and there's only one thing you can do for Him and that is learn, and learn from his disciples and his descendants that are on earth. If you have a problem, you can go to him.

Steve then told of a time at Bethany Academy of Christian Living when he prayed that there would be some money when he was short of funds, and a few days later, there was the money.

However, not everything was rosy at Bethany. There was the time that he took the Lord's name in vain: "I was smacked a couple of times for saying the Lord's name in vain . . . in front of the pastor . . . on the face. They believe in paddling. I was paddled enough to where I learned to respect [the pastor] and believe what he said."

At Bethany, Steve came to believe that God is the Almighty. There is no visible image of God's face, according to Steve. Instead, there is a shadow, like any other shadow, "that follows me around and pushes me to do right." During one talk, Steve declared that the shadow was looking over his shoulder, or both shoulders, even though Satan was on one of the shoulders. God's shadow is "stronger than" Satan's shadow, though the two get into a war sometimes.

Unlike God, Satan has some physical characteristics: "Satan is red . . . a torn-up face with horns coming out of his head. More or less a bull with a face and all of his fiery angels around him."

Jesus is all heart to Steve: "I see Jesus as a sacrifice. I see Jesus' blood." To Steve, Jesus sacrificed his life so that all "men could live under God and believe in salvation, and come live with Him at the time of their death." Jesus is all over, but mostly located in his heart.

The function of the Holy Spirit or the Holy Ghost is a combination of the Father and the Son. The Holy Spirit functions as an army "to defeat Satan," says Steve. In Steve's worldview, there is a constant battle going on, right where we live: "I think the Holy Spirit and God and Jesus are setting the battle ground right now. [The Holy Spirit] is pulling an army of Christians, and the people who are with Satan will be destroyed."

How does Steve know all of the army plans? "If the Holy Spirit wasn't in me and God and Jesus wasn't in me, I wouldn't be talking about them, because I wouldn't want to represent them if I didn't know about them." Steve truly believes that the reason that he knows all this is because of faith, which is as follows: "Believing in Christ, and that Christ died for you so that your sins will be forgiven and so that you'll be able to go to heaven when it all ended."

When I asked for Steve to tell me a story of faith-in-action, he told about his imminent release from the hospital: "I've been praying and asking to be let out of the hospital, to work toward going back to my home, and I will be leaving in one month and God has answered my prayers. I just have to keep on working." If he keeps on working in the right way, doing good works, then the Behavior Mod God will reward him with release from the hospital. While Steve acknowledged that God did some work to get to this point in his life, he is adamant that he had to do most of the work *with* God. He declared that this decision to work with God was a conscious choice of his own free will.

A common theme in much of Steve's theological worldview is focused attention on each individual doing good works on this earth in order for us to simply get God's attention and recognition. Otherwise, God is blind to our existence. Steve believes that we are called to reach out to God in enabling God to do what God's job is to do: provide salvation. Salvation totally depends upon each person. If we individually do what is right, what God expects of us, then God will reward us richly; if we do not do what God expects of us, then we will be Satan's property, says Steve. This is the mechanics of justification for a Behavior Mod God.

For example, consider this interaction regarding Steve's favorite verses in the Bible, all coming from the New Testament, Revelation 3:20: "Listen! I am standing at the door, knocking; if you hear my voice and open the door, I will come in to you, and eat with you, and you with me:"[1]

> When I was studying that verse . . . I take it to mean that God is knocking at your door constantly and it's your choice to open the door and accept Him into your heart so you can be saved.

Steve said that he found this verse when he found salvation at Bethany Academy of Christian Living. Who built the door of the house? Steve said that God did. I asked why God did not just open the door up, Steve said that that choice was ours to make. Once we open the door, then God gives us the grand prize of eternal life and salvation. These things are contingent upon each person asking God for forgiveness. Thus sanctification is not based upon God's actions, but solely on an individual's actions and responses in life. Nowhere in Steve's theological worldview is the church mentioned.

Yet the work does not stop there: you have to keep on working, "because God will help you *only* if you help yourself. In order to be saved, you have to work, [like] asking for forgiveness and helping other people out." Is there anything else that we have to do besides work? "Pray and believe, I guess," said Steve.

For Steve, he hopes that his stay at this institution will be the last of many false starts and real stops. What would he like to do when he leaves these institutions? He would like to work as a gardener or landscape artist. He does not want a college degree, though his family had high hopes that Steve was going to be the one to go to college and become a college professor. He knows he has let them down with his choice of occupation, but he says he does not really care. His desires in life are simple: he wants to pass his General Education Degree (GED), and get on with life. For Christmas, all he wanted was a pack of cigarettes, a chance to go to church, and an opportunity to walk around by himself.

. . .

For Steve, the Behavior Mod God is firmly seated in heaven, watching and hearing us, counting and graphing our good acts on the large tablet of matrix paper in the Book of Life, while Satan is doing the same, counting our bad acts, with praise coming our way from one or the other, depending on the context and intentions of our actions. If we are bad, then we get paddled, and salvation is not ours to have or receive from God. If we are good, then God smiles and opens up one of the doors of life, and lets us take a look at salvation in the visionary dream of peaceful heaven, our goal in life.

Steve's theological worldview is an excellent example of how God is perceived by many other children and adolescents with behavioral and emotional problems ruled by behavioral programming in other institutions. While they may be persecuted by abuse at home, in their short life they have also become the persecutors, committing crimes and abusive acts upon other people around them. All that holds such children and adolescents back from creating further chaos is this powerful, simplistic yet all-controlling, all-judging image of the Behavior Mod God.

What is missing from this narrative of good works is any sense of the reality of God's gift of grace shared among a community of Christians. There is no sense of rest, of comfort, or anyone sharing the yoke of life with Steve as a result of such grace. Instead, one must work, and work hard, in order to ensure that paradise is definitely in one's future.

What Steve is also robbed of in this worldview is the strength, care, love, and support of the Christian community. Steve understands that he is all alone in this pilgrimage of faith. He has no one else to talk to about the issues of the Christian faith, like salvation. Though he reads the Bible, he does so in solitary confinement. Steve believes that salvation and justification are awarded to each individual based upon each person's accumulation of good works. There is nothing much that the community can do at this point, for God judges us by our point sheet. There is little mentioned about community worship or any other ritual to guide his life; no prayer group to pray for him; no one to care for his wounds but himself at this time.

And what about the nature of God in Steve's theological worldview? God's behavior is predictable and controllable by simply satisfying God's demands upon us on the great scorecard and points system of the universe. By loving our neighbors as ourselves, following the ten commandments, honoring father and mother, not stealing, not committing adultery (Exodus 20); by following the laws in Leviticus, then God will look at our daily point sheet, and give us so many points for our good works, and sooner or later a trip to the heavenly point store for meeting the criteria for the days of our life. If we keep on meeting the criteria for good behavior throughout the days of our lives, then we are promised that God will abide by God's word and fulfill all our wishes in life. Thus God's behavior is predictable and knowable: if we are good people and do good things, then God will be good to us.

Fortunately, this cosmological behavioral plan that these young people are conditioned to believe in is not the way of God. Through active intervention throughout human history, Jews and Christians alike have wrestled and fought against the truth that God created creation, including us human creatures who inhabit the earth.[2] Sin is the reverse of this proclamation: the human creatures created creation and God in *our* image. In the stories of Job and the parables told by Jesus, God tries to get it across to humankind that God is not a creation of *our* collective imagination, but we are a creation of God's divine inspiration and imagination. It is God who holds us in the palm of God's hand, and not we who hold God in the palm of our hands, as these adolescent behaviorists would sometimes argue.

In spite of all the drastic limitations and errant theological assumptions about the nature of the Behavior Mod God, it is impressive that, given Steve's background, Steve believes in God. For all that has kept Steve's life together throughout all the institutional programs and experiences at home has been his faith and love of God. It has been Steve's belief in God that has given him the courage to survive the harrowing ordeals that he has confronted in his short life. And it is by God's gift of grace through faith that will lead Steve home to God.

23

Randy's Coat
of Many Colors

O ne of the most powerful, dramatic ways that people may show
care and love toward one another is by sharing stories with other
people, especially when someone is in need of a story that provides
hope and guidance in life. In his story, *Crow and Weasel* (1991), the
writer Barry Lopez captures the vital power of sharing stories in our
lives, a need which is so strong and so essential that sometimes we
need stories more than we need food to stay alive:

> Remember only this one thing: the stories people tell have a way
> of taking care of them. If stories come to you, care for them. And
> learn to give them away where they are needed. Sometimes a per-
> son needs a story more than food to stay alive. That is why we
> put these stories in each other's memory. This is how people care
> for themselves.[1]

Why are stories so important to all people? Embedded and woven in
the very fabric of stories we tell and listen, express and receive, is all
the information we need in order to not only live and survive, but to
actually thrive in this world. For the stories connect us human beings,
all of whom are social beings, with other people, places, and times.
Because of this connection with others in the sharing of stories we
are able to navigate through the new, often uncharted, chaotic and
extraordinary moments that are directly behind us as well as looming
before us.

The reason that stories are such a powerful influence in our lives is because to be human is to not only have and tell a story, but to *be* a story. It is natural for human beings to communicate with one another through the stories we wish to tell and long to hear in the midst of our primary communities of meaning, as in our families and churches.[2] It is through and by stories that we share that we know the world in general, and our religious communities in particular. And it is through the stories that we share in our churches and synagogues about God's salvific acts that hold a people together in the moments of exhilaration or grief in the present because of what God has done in the past. The master or sacred story of God that Jews and Christians alike are embedded in, surrounded by, and guided by, which is told and celebrated in a myriad of ways, enables our respective communities of faith to get their bearing. This then provides a glimpse of the meaning of life, which is integral for God's people to exist and thrive in this world.

In the very act of placing or embedding our individual stories in the larger, enveloping context of God's story, we declare that we are no longer spinners of our own, individual, isolated stories. Instead, our life stories are collectively spun out of this often mysterious yet real and true sacred narrative of God that has preceded us for generations. It is unfolding in our midst today among God's people in this world.

In my work with children at this hospital, I have witnessed this spinning process in the act of giving and receiving stories, a true act of a caring relationship between two people. The storyteller of this chapter is Randy, a young boy of twelve who has a history of emotional problems, has been identified as being somewhat delayed in his cognitive growth, has most likely witnessed sexual abuse in his own family, who is in search of a home and a family he can call his own. One of the very reasons that he is still at this hospital is because his parents are not able to care for him, and his biological sister is too young to take him into her home. He is one of the many pilgrims that I have met at this place.

I have been amazed at the power of stories in Randy's life. He introduced himself to me after I read a children's story on his unit. I cannot remember the story that I read at that time, but what I remembered is that he really liked stories. He liked not only listening to them, but telling and retelling them and discussing them as well, which was unusual compared to his friends on the unit.

For example, consider the story of *Jack and the Dragaman*, one of the Jack Tales told in the southeastern states. The story revolves around the escapades of a young man, Jack, who is interested in finding out who, or what, is this strange man who keeps on disturbing his family every time he and his brothers sit down to eat a dinner in their newly built cabin. One day, after the shocking appearance of this strange man, Jack follows this strange man down a hole in the earth, discovering that this character is no ordinary man but a dragonlike man, the Dragaman, who blows fire and smoke. Within his living quarters, there are these lovely women, one of whom Jack plans to marry. After much trickery and chicanery, Jack is able to vanquish the Dragaman and save his bride-to-be, bringing her to safety in his cabin.

I told the story to the children on Randy's unit. From outward appearances, Randy listened to the story attentively, though I did not know how much or how well he had listened to the story. Unbeknownst to me, in the coming days he began to really take apart the story in his mind, rewriting bits and pieces so that he was included in the narrative, drew a picture for the retelling of this story, retitled the story *Fire Dragon*, and surprised me with it one day, with a cover and all:

Fire Dragon

One day in a jungle there were people living there and from a big mountain there were fire balls. Randy, Peter, and Jon came back from the [Civil] War and they built a house. One day Randy made a pie and other foods, and then the door got knocked down. This Big Man came in and ate all of the food and then he was gone. The next day Peter made lots of food, then the big man came and ate all of the food up, and then the next day Randy said to the Big Man, "Come to our house and eat dinner with us," and the Big Man said "No thanks." Then he went to the mountain and I was behind him. Then he went into the hole. Peter said "If there is a Big Man, get his gold." Then I went down the rope and I went in the hole. It was dark, then I saw a very big house. I saw a very nice lady who said, "If you save me you have to kill the Fire Dragon." Then the lady gave me a knife, a wise ring, and fire water. She said good-bye. There is a rope up there: go up it. Then he seen the Fire Dragon, he turned into a dragon, then he put fire on me. Then I put water on me and the burn went away. Then I stabbed with the knife then he turned into a ball of fire and went away. I saw all of the gold. I put some of the gold in a big bag. I ran to the rope . . . it wasn't there, so I said, "I wish I was at my house, and my ring put me at my house." Then I saw that nice lady, and I put a bow in her hair. We made a new house and had kids. And then we lived a happy life.

Though parts of the story are roughly retold, nevertheless Randy had not only listened, but feasted upon and taken in the story so well that he, himself, reconfigured the story that it became his to tell and share with others as the original storyteller. Randy was no longer a story listener: he had crossed the invisible yet real line of becoming a storyteller.

For a few months, Randy was satisfied with just coming to the unit time of reading stories. Then one day, Randy brought me an old paperback book, which was a retelling of the story of the biblical character Joseph and his coat of many colors (based upon Genesis 37–50).[3] Why did Randy bring me this story? Simply because he liked the story of this young boy who was abandoned by his family. However, this story meant more to him than he first admitted, for it became his story, one that he could relate to well. For like Joseph, Randy too felt abandoned by his family, left to fend for himself within the confines of this institution.

Our first reading of this book occurred in the late afternoon by the lakeside at the hospital, the sun beginning to set. We were only going to read one chapter, but the time shared together was so rich, we splurged and read three whole chapters. The pattern for reading a chapter was that I would read a page, then he would read a page, and we would alternate between the two of us. Having a reading disability, Randy stumbled over many of the words, but he was insistent that he wanted to go on and read the story aloud. After each chapter we read, we talked about the significance of Joseph's story in his life. Randy admitted that the reason he liked this story so much is because he and Joseph have a lot in common: like Joseph who was abandoned by his brothers and left for sale to strangers, Randy has often felt abandoned by his parents. Like Joseph who had to make a home in a strange land in order to survive, Randy has also had to make it in a strange land of the institution in order to survive. In a very concrete sense, Randy placed his life story into the context of God's sacred story as revealed in the biblical story of Joseph. By doing so, Randy discovered and gained new insight into his own life situation. He gained some confidence that, like Joseph, God was going to do something wondrous and new with him. What was most important was that he was learning more about who he is through the knowledge of whose he is: like Joseph, he is one of God's children. We finally stopped reading *not* because Randy did not want to read anymore, but the sunlight had been replaced by the full moon of the evening.

New insights and revelations to himself about himself came with each reading of Joseph's story. For example, after reading about the promises and lies people like Potiphar's wife told about Joseph, our discussion had to do with the promises and lies we have told in life. I asked Randy if he had ever promised or lied to someone before:

> I have promised and sometimes, when I promise [something] to somebody I'll forget and when it comes up, I'll say "I forgot." Sometimes I'll do that.

Had Randy ever lied before?

> A few times . . . When I was young at another place I [was] framed for something another body did. People kept on me so . . . I said I did it. I lied once or twice.

I reminded Randy about the importance of honesty in Joseph's story. Randy admitted that he was like Joseph, because he has felt at times that people were against him, like Joseph's brothers were against him.

In another session we talked about the prison scene in Joseph's story, where Joseph was locked away with the chief cupbearer and the chief baker. Randy could truly empathize with this part of the story because he feels that he is in prison while living in this institution. What is he waiting for? "Freedom . . . from jail . . . from life of behaviorism . . . [and freedom to go] home, my life." Randy's hopeful dream is that someday, someone will come and take him home.

In one of our final sessions, we finished the story of Joseph, when his brothers arrived in Egypt and begged for food from one of the leaders in Egypt who was really Joseph. It was soon after this begging session that Joseph revealed to his brothers who he was: not only was he a leading figure in Egypt, but he was their brother, Joseph. Randy smiled throughout the dramatic points of this part of the story of revelation and honesty.

I asked Randy what would God tell him to do if he were the wisest person on his unit: "God is telling me to be the one to show a [good] example." He talked about how hard it is to be a good example to the other children on the unit. What was surprising was that even this admission of sharing his opinions was an exciting revelation for Randy, because he has rarely expressed his thoughts and feelings with others before.

In our last session together, we talked about Joseph's brothers having to go to Egypt where there was plenty of grain to feed them while they are starving. We read about Joseph forgiving his brothers for the wrong that they did in harming him and selling him to strangers. And we smiled at the happy reunion at the conclusion of this long story.

I asked Randy what was the moral point of Joseph's story:

> Even though you're jealous of somebody else, [like] your brothers, don't get jealous. [We get jealous] sometimes because we don't have the stuff other people have.

Who is the hero of this story? "Joseph," he says. I asked him if he is a modern-day Joseph, and Randy smiles and enthusiastically says "Yes!" Does God use this story to help us learn about living with one another? Randy acknowledges that we learn in this story the impor- tance of care for others, and that God is watching and listening for the moments we learn to forgive each other when we have hurt some- one. God likes it when we live in such a state of forgiveness.

Two weeks later, Randy is discharged from the hospital, off to live in a less restrictive place. In talking to his therapist, I found out later that Randy had become more comfortable with himself in the last few months, talking loudly and acting out among others. While on the one hand, the therapist was not sure that she liked the "new" Randy, we both recognized that Randy was acting more like a twelve-year-old child. The awkward, still silence with which he surrounded himself for the first months in this hospital began to fall away like scales as he became more comfortable with himself and his place in the life of the hospital. The new therapist has the task of finding a foster home for Randy.

• • •

In the Gospel of Mark 4:33–34, it is recorded that Jesus taught people about God and the kingdom of heaven primarily by using parables: "With many such parables he spoke the word to them, as they were able to hear it; he did not speak to them except in parables." As has been shown throughout other parts of the gospel, Jesus truly understood the limits of our mortal human condition and how we best understand the world. While we may not understand the abstract, theoretical explanations of the nature of God, often feeling more confused and bewildered than enlightened by such discussions, there is something about the telling and hearing, the mutual sharing of a story, especially God's story, that speaks clearly to our hearts and minds.

Randy is one among many children who best understand the world in general, and God in particular, through story. He is dependent upon the stories of life in order to make heads or tales of his predicament in this hospital.

By literally placing his solitary life story into the context of God's story, as revealed in the Joseph narrative found in the book of Genesis, Randy rediscovers that he, like Joseph, has not been left alone after all. God was watching over Joseph, from the moments of his playing on the hillside while watching sheep, to being left in the pit for sale, the anxiety of prison life in a strange land, and the mixture of hope and bitterness in being reunited with his brothers who first wished to lose him. God is watching over Randy, from his days as a child with his mother and father, to his isolation inside an institution, to the hopeful reunification with his family and the outside neighborhood.

By listening and taking Randy's story seriously, I witnessed Randy's story of life being spun out through the sacred narrative of Joseph. In sharing stories with one another, Randy knows that he was cared for by another friend. By sharing with Randy the time of reading the Joseph narrative, Randy has found a primary narrative that gives him hope, faith, and a sense of God's love, even amid institutional living. He has taken upon himself Joseph's coat of many colors. In this sharing of stories, Randy knows that his life story is important, has been taken seriously, and that he has a place, an identity, a sense of self that is grounded in the sacred, eternally relevant narrative of God's protective love for all God's children.

Epilogue
Being a Spiritual Dude:
Lessons from Living
with Disabled Adolescents

All was quiet among the young people on a unit in a hospital for adolescents with behavioral problems, before I entered through the doors. The moment I unlocked the second door and stepped out into the unit, Dan saw me. Upon seeing me, Dan, one of the young people at the hospital, let out a loud, "Hey, Spiritual Dude!" The rest of the young people and staff on the unit laughed a good-natured laugh, and with that I am named, or better yet christened, by the young people of this hospital. No longer am I pastor, chaplain, counselor, or the ethicist: the young people consider me their Spiritual Dude.

In 1991, I began working full-time as the Director of Religious Life in this institution for children and adolescents with behavioral disorders. While the job description called for me to be many things to many people, the young people of the hospital perceived me as one thing: their Spiritual Dude. Working at a hospital where only the Director of Religious Life can talk with the children and adolescents about God and other religious experiences, has given me entree into a world of stories that has left me far richer than when I first came to this hospital and this position. It was hard to leave these children in January 1993.

Gaining entry into the lives of these young people, being given permission to receive and, later on, to bear, the dramatic and comedic narratives of their lives was gained by basically *being with* the young people on their turf, which comprises the hospital unit and the school. This in itself is a challenge for many educators and pastors who are prone to doing something *to* or to work *on* someone else. But beginning with the approach of merely being with them, though frightening at the start, became easier as time went on. What I gained by this quiet approach was the trust among the young people and unit staff.

Being with the young people in an institution that has never had a pastoral counselor or religious educator on its staff was new for everyone. Not pressing an explicit, overt agenda was also something novel for the young people, because every day they are called to dutifully fulfill the prearranged goals and objectives of health care professionals: special educators, psychiatrists, psychologists, nurses, social workers, and therapists, to name a few. Yet I also had a telos in mind in taking this approach: to be open to discover what the religious experiences were of the young people whom society had labeled "a behavior disorder."

Society at large, which crafted the labels and categories that later assigned these young people to this hospital, broadly defines a behavior disorder as one of these four characteristics: some children have a conduct disorder, demonstrating outwardly angry defiance and hostility toward all authority figures; some are anxious and withdrawn from groups of people; others are immature, with an air of ambiguity about everything and anything that happens around them; finally others are "socialized aggressive," a lifestyle shaped and nurtured when hanging around gangs.

These clinical definitions reflect how the world around us often wants us to think about and treat these young people: as objects who are to be dissected and manipulated in a way that gives *us*, the professionals, power over *them*, the children with behavior disorders. Seeing these children as a composite of data, an intellectual problem, a series of dots, dashes, and graph paper on a behavioral chart, someone who has to be controlled and made predictable in order to fit an understanding of the world, removes that which is essentially human about the child with a disability. The child with a disability becomes an objective problem rather than a child who is hurting, abused, and in need of love. The labels we use in describing a condition complete their objective of hiding rather than revealing the person.

While the labels and categories of society tell us how someone did on a professional's assessment tool, information that is helpful in rather limited and narrowly defined experiences, the labels fail to tell us either *who* the child is or, more important, *whose* the child is. Listening to the stories of these young people fills in the gaps between the dry, narrow, and often superfluous definitions of the labels and categories of a disability in need of a context. While the world often sees the young disabled person as needing to be predictably controlled by the assigned labels and therapeutic specialists, the Christian community envisions this child in a radically different way, given the alternative worldview that is claimed and lived out among those in the body of Christ: each child is created in the image of God (Gen. 1:27). As one of God's children, these young people have tasted, tried out, and have pushed against the borders of the human condition and the social context where they live. They often go beyond the rational, logical borders and the accepted norms of society, which in the end brings such children to an institution.

To say that life has been difficult for many of these young people sounds almost trite and simplistic; besides, there has been enough reductionistic and simplistic thinking about a child's complex problems by pigeonholing them into a label and category. Life itself, in all its beauty as well as brutality, has been the force that has pushed these children to be so fully human. Any romantic notions of the human condition, with mistaken beliefs that they are pure, angelic innocence and embody saintly honesty is quickly destroyed when interacting with these young people. There is a hungry, raw energy within many of them. Others have a calloused, hardworn toughness around the edges, which often comes from one too many fights with someone in authority that they have either won or lost. Some are so sullen and withdrawn one wishes they would be more agitated and reactive to what has happened in their lives filled with abuse and callous disregard.

What happens in being silent and still, hearing and listening to the stories in the midst of the swirling chaotic actions of the children on a unit, for once allowing the young person to be the initiator, mentor, and teacher while the other is a student, is that the person *behind* the label comes forth. Suddenly, new insights and lessons of life are shared. In listening to their stories from life, these young people, with their labels of one disabling condition or another, sound more and more human. They reveal the sweetness and the savagery of the human condition because of what they have experienced in life.

For example, consider these stories: there is one, quietly angry African-American young man who has assaulted people with guns and knives in order to survive life amid the chaotic gang warfare on the streets of one of our inner cities. There is the uppity young African-American woman who, at the age of thirteen, had an abortion; there are several young women who were raped, some at the tender age of three, who still ask for sexual favors from the other young people and the staff, because this is the only way that they know how to get what they want in the world. There is the depressed, young, Anglo-American boy, who has been addicted to drugs since he was six years old because his mother, who thought drugs helped her in life, believed that it would help her son as well. And there are the shy, if not sullen, young boys and girls who have been taken away from the families, homes, and neighborhoods where they used to ride their bicycles late into the night, because they were physically abused at the age of five, or their mother and father abandoned them, and their aging grandmothers could no longer keep them at home; they are lonely and long to be with a family, preferably their own family and not a foster family.

The reaction of many people to the tangible, real pain of these young people has been outright rejection, not loving acceptance. The pain that these young people represent and live from shoots holes in the already battle-worn fabric of society. Such pain tears human families and communities apart, leaving them in tatters, which take ages to mend. Families want to distance themselves from these children: their natural, step, or foster families do not want them, leaving them on the doorsteps of jails and institutions. The public and private schools do not want them, for in the midst of shrinking federal and state budgets for special education, these young people cost too much for remedial services that probably will not make a difference in their lives. Publicly funded community mental health centers in our inner cities are stretched beyond their human capacities in terms of what they can handle and provide the ever-growing number of cases. Finally, churches and their associated youth groups do not want these young people in their congregations or youth activities. While some churches find it possible to provide some pity and often patronizing phrases for those with other disabling conditions, like physical disabilities and mental retardation, children and adolescents with behavioral disorders are too much for the church. Their searing pain is too much for the trivial pity that churches are used to dishing out to the disenfranchised. Besides, what these children need and want is not paltry pity, but the radical, refreshing, life-giving love of God in Christ. In the Christian community is the love that can heal the deep wounds in their angry hearts, transforming the anger that slices others to the quick into an ethereal yet earthy joy that is efficacious in nature.

What the young people are waiting for and depending on is someone to not only say but act on the good news of God's love. This is not "tough love" or "justice love," as some groups are wont to claim. To quote the African-American spiritual and Old Testament reference, God's love is the healing balm of Gilead, that "makes the wounded whole" and "heals the sin-sick soul." The mysterious part of this story is that somehow or other, these children have a hunch, an inkling of faith, believing that God's love may do something that not even the best thought-out behavior plan and most effective medication can touch. These tools of modern science can only touch the surface, not the core, of our being. They know, as they brood, nag, glare, and suffer with their hurt and wounded pride on the unit, that they are being pursued by God's love.

Consider these stories that reveal the slightest glimmers of faith in God and agape love: Burt, a young man with Tourette's[1] syndrome asked me this question: "What if God asked me, 'If you could be anyone or anything in this world, what would you be?' I think I'd tell God that I want to be me, all of me, with my limitations and all, because it has made me the person I am and I like who I am, thank you very much."

Or remember George, the young boy who is mentally retarded and hyperactive. At a recent worship service by the lakeside at the hospital, there was a reading from the prophet Amos, chapter 5, verse 24: "But let justice roll down like waters, and righteousness like an everflowing stream." Without any questions or evocation, George pointed to the lake and volunteered to the group that God's justice is just like those waters "over there, like our lake, they never stop, do they?"

Remember the plaintive cry of Ben, who is a poet in his heart of hearts. Though his rhyming patterns and words may strike some as being juvenile at best, living in the midst of such controlled oppression, it is amazing to consider his thoughts uniquely expressed in his own poetry:

> As I try to find peace
>   in a world of war;
> As I search for sanity
>   where there is no more.

And even if the fools of this world
who shape our society
cannot see the meaning in my work,
For all God's grace,
let Him guide me to a better place.

Elsewhere, think about the story of Stephanie, the young woman who is an artist, who is feeling lonely, isolated, and often unwanted by her family who have grown weary of her histrionics in seeking attention for her hurting wounds. One day, after visiting home for a week, and returning to a unit where there was little concern or attention given to her, she struck out, even mistakenly hitting me in the face as she was swinging at another girl ("Turning Cheeks").

Later on, talking about the incident, Stephanie said that the punch was not meant for me or the other girl, but for God: she wanted to punch God's lights out! Out of her fear of being isolated, she eloquently yelled at me and God: "God has left me all alone . . . where is he? Huh? Jesus has left me all alone . . . where is he? Huh? Where is your God? Where is your Jesus when I am hurting inside and my prayers are left unattended upon the altar of God? Tell me where your God is when I'm hurting so bad?"

There is Kendall, another young man who has Tourette's syndrome. He is new to a unit, fearful of the larger, angrier young people, but nonetheless in much need of God's love. One day when I was walking on the unit, he was in his room crying. Why was he crying? "Because I have no friends here. Everyone is so loud and demanding. I'm very lonely and have no friends here; no one will listen to me, not even God."

One day, Margaret, a young woman of fifteen who lived on a habit of drugs and sex on the streets in one of our inner cities, caught me by the arm and sat me down in her room. She had to read to me one of her journal entries, because it concerned her faith in God:

> Well, I know this man named God Almighty. He really helped me do very good some days. I will come to his Kingdom someday soon. I [would] like to go and have fun with my King, God Almighty.
>
> I have done some bad things in my lifetime, and I have paid for my mistakes, and when I have really paid for my mistakes I have got something good out of it, and I say "Thank you God Almighty, for letting me really see my mistakes."

After reading the letter, in a shy manner Margaret shared with me that she makes it each day, living on the hope and in faith that God really loves her and forgives her, "doesn't he, Dr. Brett?" I told her God truly loves her as we closed with the Lord's Prayer, prayed in unison.

Finally, there is Isaac, who is as tough as they come in looks as well as demeanor. He is usually quiet on the unit, though everyone understands that he has led a dangerous life on the city streets before being sent to prison, and then shipped off to this institution. When riding home in my car from a trip to the mall, he shared how he has been touched by God: "When I was at home, I went with my grandmother to church, the House of Prayer. I don't know why, but I always cry when I go to church, like when they sing the song 'This Little Light of Mine,' and 'Bless the Lord, Oh my Soul.' I just don't know why, but I bawl like a baby when I hear those songs. Even when I was in prison and would go to chapel, I would cry." We quietly sang these songs in my car until we arrive back at the institution, and then both of us were silent.

In the midst of the ugliness of institutional life, something beautiful is growing. Like a rose that surprises everyone as it rises unexpectedly in the midst of great, choking thorns, these stories emerge from the hurting and abusive lives of these children in a most unexpected place. One can only imagine how these stories would grow in an environment of overwhelming trust, generous care, ever-present hope, genuine faith, and godly compassion. One becomes sensitive to the subtle signs of God's presence in the lives of these young people. Yet, once you have seen it, and begin to develop sensitivity to these signs, they are hard to miss and exciting to watch unfold before one's very eyes. Being a Spiritual Dude does not make one master of these narratives. Instead, this role makes one humble in understanding the rarest gift that is being given by God through these children: the gift of one's life story from one person to another, being witness to the presence of God in these fragile yet toughened human stories in an otherwise unholy setting.

Notes

Introduction:
A Journey of Seeing

1. Norman Maclean, *A River Runs Through It* (New York: Simon and Schuster, 1992), p. 69.

2. All the names in this book have been changed for the reason of confidentiality.

3. Evelyn Fox Keller, *A Feeling for the Organism* (New York: Freeman Publishing Company, 1983), p. 198.

Chapter 2:
Listen and Learn from Narratives
That Tell a Story

1. Sylvia Plath, *The Bell Jar* (New York: Harper and Row, 1971).

2. Christopher Nolan, *Under the Eye of the Clock* (New York: St. Martin's Press, 1987).

3. Clara Park, *The Siege* (Boston: Atlantic-Little, Brown, 1982).

4. *Living in Faith: A Resource for Teachers of Older Youth and Adults Who Are Retarded* (Nashville: Cokesbury Press, 1986).

5. Ibid., p. 5.

6. Robert Coles, *The Moral Life of Children* (Boston: Atlantic Monthly Press, 1986), pp. 10–14.

7. Robert Coles, *Moral Life of Children*, and *The Political Life of Children* (Boston: Atlantic Monthly Press, 1986).

8. Coles, *Moral Life of Children*, p. 14.

9. Coles, *Political Life of Children*, p. 17.

10. Ibid., p. 29.

11. Coles, *Moral Life of Children*, p. 4.

12. Ibid., p. 29.

13. Coles, *Political Life of Children*, p. 291.

14. Ibid., p. 40.

15. Coles, *Moral Life of Children*, p. 210.

16. Ibid., p. 154.

17. Coles, *Political Life of Children*, p. 281.

18. Ibid., p. 281.

19. Stanley Hauerwas, *Christian Existence Today* (Durham: Labyrinth Press, 1988), p. 25.

20. Victor Turner and Edward Bruner, *The Anthropology of Experience* (Chicago: University of Illinois Press, 1986), p. 140.

21. Kieran Egan, *Educational Development* (New York: Oxford University Press, 1979), p. 34.

22. Turner and Bruner, *Anthropology of Experience*, p. 145.

23. Clara Park, *Siege*, p. 144.

24. John Dominic Crossan, *The Dark Interval* (Sonoma: Polebridge Press, 1988), p. x.

25. Coles, *Moral Life of Children*, p. 15.

26. Judith Goetz and Margaret LeCompte, *Ethnography and Qualitative Design in Educational Research* (Orlando: Academic Press, 1984), p. 244.

27. George Marcus and Michael Fischer, *Anthropology as Social Critique* (Chicago: University of Chicago Press), p. 18.

28. Michael Patton, *Qualitative Evaluation Methods* (Beverley Hills: Sage Publication, 1986), p. 158.

29. Turner and Bruner, *Anthropology of Experience*, p. 146.

30. Ibid.

31. Gloria Anzaldua, "Tlilli, Tlapalli: The Path of the Red and Black Ink," in Rick Simonson and Scott Walker, *Graywolf Annual: Multi-Cultural Literacy* (St. Paul: Graywolf Press, 1988), p. 32.

Chapter 4:
A Quilt of Compassion:
The Disability-Affected Family and the Church

1. Clara Park, *The Siege* (Boston: Atlantic-Little, Brown), pp. 122–44.

2. John Gliedman and William Roth, *The Unexpected Minority: Handicapped Children in America* (New York, 1979), p. 104. This passage is found in Stanley Hauerwas, *Suffering Presence* (Notre Dame: University of Notre Dame Press, 1986), p. 189.

3. Pamela Wickham-Searl, "Mothers with a Mission," in Philip Ferguson, Dianne Ferguson, and Steven Taylor, Eds., *Interpreting Disability: A Qualitative Reader* (New York: Teachers College Press, 1992), p. 251.

4. Stanley Hauerwas, *Suffering Presence*, pp. 189–210.

5. Judith Stacey, *Brave New Families* (New York: Harper-Collins, 1990), pp. 16–19.

6. Maureen O'Hara, and Walter Truett Anderson, "Welcome to the Postmodern World," *Family Therapy Networker* 15, 5 (1991), 18–25.

7. Kenneth J. Gergen, "The Saturated Family," *The Family Therapy Networker* 15, 5 (1991), 27–35.

8. James L. Paul, *Understanding and Working with Parents of Children with Special Needs* (New York: Holt, Rinehart, and Winston, 1981), p. 19.

9. Wickham-Searl, "Mothers with a Mission," pp. 251–73.

10. Whitney Otto, *How to Make an American Quilt* (New York: Bantam, 1991).

11. Christopher Lash, *Haven in a Heartless World* (New York: Basic Books, 1977).

12. Bernard Ikeler, *Parenting Your Disabled Child* (Philadelphia: Westminster Press, 1986), pp. 13–25.

13. Hauerwas, *Suffering Presence*, pp. 189–210.

14. Harold Kushner, *When Bad Things Happen To Good People* (New York: Schocken Books, 1981).

15. Walter Brueggemann, *The Message of the Psalms: A Theological Commentary* (Minneapolis: Augsburg, 1984), p. 169.

16. Bernard Ikeler, *Parenting Your Disabled Child*, pp. 38–52.

17. Ibid., p. 39.

18. Wickham-Searl, "Mothers with a Mission," p. 270.

19. Annie Dillard, *The Living* (New York: Harper-Collins, 1992).

20. Edwin Friedman, *Generation to Generation* (New York: Guilford Press, 1985).

21. Ibid., p. 3.

22. Ibid., pp. 1–8.

23. Ibid., pp. 6, 7.

24. Carl Whitaker, Devereux Family Therapy Institute: Carl Whitaker Conference, Cocoa Beach, Florida, February 1992.

25. Friedman, *Generation to Generation*, p. 7.

26. Paul, *Understanding and Working with Parents of Children with Special Needs*, p. 1.

27. Park, *The Siege*, p. 142.

28. Hauerwas, *Suffering Presence*, pp. 211–17.

29. Ibid., p. 213.

30. Ikeler, *Parenting Your Disabled Child*, p. 103.

31. Hauerwas, *Suffering Presence*, p. 213.

32. Ikeler, *Parenting Your Disabled Child*, pp. 100–20.

33. Christopher Lasch, *The True and Only Heaven* (New York: W. W. Norton, 1991), p. 36.

Chapter 5:
The Prophetic Voice of Parents with Disabled Children

1. Frederick Buechner, *Wishful Thinking* (New York: Harper and Row, 1973), pp. 73–75.

2. Bernhard Anderson, *Understanding the Old Testament*, 3rd ed. (Englewood Cliffs: Prentice Hall Publishing Company, 1975), pp. 226–27.

Chapter 6:
Welcoming Unexpected Guests to the Banquet

1. Helen Featherstone, *There's a Difference in the Family* (New York: Penguin Books, 1981), p. 33.

2. Bernard Ikeler, *Parenting Your Disabled Child* (Philadelphia: Westminster Press, 1986), p. 17.

3. Ernest Becker, *The Denial of Death* (New York: Free Press, 1973), pp. 11–24.

4. Stanley Hauerwas, *Naming the Silences* (Grand Rapids: Wm. B. Eerdmans Publishing Co., 1990), p. 146.

5. Richard Katz, "Empowerment and Synergy: Expanding the Community's Healing Resources." Unpublished manuscript, Cambridge: Harvard University, 1984, p. 1.

6. This perception of love emerged in conversations with Stanley Hauerwas.

7. Lesslie Newbigin, *Sign of the Kingdom* (Grand Rapids: Wm. B. Eerdmans Publishing Company, 1977), pp. 69–70.

8. T. W. Manson in Joseph Fitzmyer, *Anchor Bible Commentary: The Gospel According to Luke, X-XXIV* (New York: Doubleday, 1985), p. 1054.

9. John Howard Yoder, *The Priestly Kingdom* (Notre Dame: University of Notre Dame Press, 1984), pp. 80–101.

10. Wendell Berry, *Home Economics* (San Francisco: North Point Press, 1987), pp. 112–22.

Chapter 7:
Pilgrims Lost in an Alien Land

1. Stanley Hauerwas and L. Gregory Jones, *Why Narrative?* (Grand Rapids: Wm. B. Eerdmans Publishing Company, 1989), p. 12.

2. A behavioral disorder means a condition exhibiting one or more of the following characteristics over a long period of time and to a marked degree, which adversely affects educational performance: (a) an inability to learn which cannot be explained by intellectual, sensory, or health factors; (b) an inability to build or maintain satisfactory interpersonal relationships with peers and teachers; (c) inappropriate types of behavior or feelings under normal circumstances; (d) a general pervasive mood of unhappiness or depression; or (e) a tendency to develop physical symptoms or fears associated with personal or school problems. (*Federal Register*, vol. 42, no. 163[1977]: 42478, as amended in *Federal Register*, vol. 46 [1981]:3866).

3. Betty Epanchin and James L. Paul, *Emotional Problems of Childhood and Adolescence: A Multidisciplinary Approach* (Columbus: Merrill Publishing Company, 1987), pp. 14–29.

4. Christopher Lasch, *The True and Only Heaven* (New York: W. W. Norton, 1991), p. 15.

5. Epanchin and Paul, *Emotional Problems*, p. 23.

6. John Bunyan, *Pilgrim's Progress* (Laurel, New York: Lightyear Press, 1984).

7. Barry Lopez, *Crossing Open Ground* (New York: Vintage Press, 1988), p. 68.

8. Geoffrey Chaucer, *Canterbury Tales* (New York: Bantam Press, 1982), p. 3.

9. Bunyan, *Pilgrim's Progress*.

10. Avi, "The True Confessions of Charlotte Doyler," in *The Hornbook* 68, 1 (1992), 27.

11. Lopez, *Crossing Open Ground*, p. 69.

12. Ibid., p. 70.

13. Dr. James Paul helped with this concept.

Chapter 8:
A Poet Among Us

1. Bernhard Anderson, *Out of the Depths* (Philadelphia: Westminster Press, 1974), p.1.

Chapter 9:
Finding God in Motley Crue

1. Annie Dillard, *Holy the Firm* (New York: Harper Colophon Books, 1977), p. 59.

Chapter 10:
Turning Cheeks

1. The institution taught all staff who worked with these children the basic crisis prevention and intervention moves. The philosophy behind this approach is to protect both the child, who is violent, as well as other people around the child so that no one is physically hurt. It is intended to be a nonviolent approach to controlling a child who is physically aggressive.

Chapter 12:
The Religious Narratives of Disabled Adolescents

1. William Meissner, "The Phenomenology of Religious Psychopathology," *Bulletin of the Menninger Clinic* 55, 3 (1991), 281–98.

2. Peter Gay, *Freud: A Life for Our Time* (New York: W. W. Norton, 1988), p. 526.

3. Sigmund Freud, *Future of an Illusion* (New York: W. W. Norton, 1961), pp. 30–31.

4. Ana-Maria Rizzuto, *The Birth of the Living God* (Chicago: University of Chicago Press, 1979), pp. 177–211.

5. Jean Piaget, *The Child's Conception of the World* (Totowa, N.J.: Littlefield, Adams Quality Paperback, 1979), p. 268.

6. Robert Schalock, "Appropriate Supports," unpublished manuscript of classification in mental retardation, Washington, D.C.: AAMR, 1991.

7. The formal interview questions were part of an ethnographic study of the Religious Narrative Research Project.

8. Robert Coles, *The Spiritual Life of Children* (Boston: Houghton Mifflin, 1990), p. 22.

9. John Dewey, *A Common Faith* (New Haven: Yale University Press, 1934), pp. 1–28.

10. Stanley Hauerwas, *A Peaceable Kingdom* (Notre Dame: University of Notre Dame Press, 1983), p. xvi.

11. Garrett Green, *Imagining God* (New York: Harper & Row, 1989), p. 99.

12. Alisdair MacIntyre, *After Virtue*, 2nd Edition (Notre Dame: University of Notre Dame Press, 1984), p. 205.

13. Jerome Bruner, *Acts of Meaning* (Cambridge: Harvard University, 1990), p. 111.

14. MacIntyre, *After Virtue*, pp. 211–12.

15. George Howard, "Cultural Tales: A Narrative Approach to Thinking, Cross-Cultural Psychology, and Psychotherapy," *American Psychologist* 46, 3 (1991), 187–97.

16. MacIntyre, *After Virtue*, p. 219.

17. James Fowler, *Stages of Faith* (San Francisco: Harper & Row, 1981).

Chapter 14:
The Religious Imagination of Disabled Children

1. Diane Ackerman, *A Natural History of the Senses* (New York: Random House, 1990), p. xviii.

2. Ibid., p. xviii.

3. John Eccles and David Robinson, *The Wonder of Being Human* (Boston: New Science Library, 1985), p. 33.

4. Ackerman, *Natural History of Senses*, p. xix.

5. Robin Barrow, "Some Observations on the Concept of Imagination," in Kieran Egan and Dan Nadaner, *Imagination and Education* (New York: Teachers College Press, 1988), pp. 79–90.

6. In looking at what is "religious" in these narratives, Robert Coles's *The Spiritual Life of Children* (Boston: Houghton Mifflin, 1990), Garrett Green's *Imagining God* (San Francisco: Harper and Row, 1989), and John Dewey's *A Common Faith* (New Haven: Yale University Press, 1934) were consulted. What these three writers left out was the primary role of the religious or faith community, which is largely responsible for being and becoming the sacred place in which these impressions of God were made upon the lives of these children.

7. Stanley Hauerwas, *A Peaceable Kingdom* (Notre Dame: University of Notre Dame Press, 1983), p. 156.

8. Roberta Martin, *R as in Chrrristopher* (Portland: Alcuin Press, 1990).

9. Richard Wilbur, "For Dudley," in Edward Robinson, *Language of Mystery* (London: SCM Press, 1987), p. 5.

10. Robinson, *Language of Mystery*, pp. 5–14.

11. John Dewey, *Art as Experience* (New York: Capricorn Books, 1958), pp. 35–57.

12. Brian Sutton-Smith, "In Search of the Imagination," in Kieran Egan and Dan Nadaner, *Imagination and Education* (New York: Teachers College Press, 1988); Mary Warnock, *Imagination* (Berkeley: University of California Press, 1978); Edward Robinson, *Language of Mystery*.

13. Elliot Eisner, *The Educational Imagination* (New York: Macmillan Press, 1985), pp. 175–91.

Chapter 15:
Pictures of God ... At an Institution

1. Rudolf Arnheim, *To The Rescue of Art* (Berkeley: University of California Press), pp. 17–18.

2. John Dixon, *Art and the Theological Imagination* (New York: Seabury Press, 1978), pp. 130–59.

3. Ibid., pp. 1–17.

4. Ibid., p. 12.

Chapter 17
Holy Surprises

1. Uri Shulevitz, *Toddlecreek Post Office* (New York: Farrar, Strauss, & Giroux, 1990).

Chapter 18:
George's Encounter with the Lord: An Adventure

1. The title for this chapter was chosen by George.

2. Uta Frith, *Autism: Explaining the Enigma* (Oxford: Basil Blackwell, 1989), p. 60, found in Judy Barron and Sean Barron, *There's a Boy in Here* (New York: Simon & Schuster, 1992).

Chapter 20:
The Importance of Stories in Acts of Caring

1. Barry Lopez, *Winter Count* (New York: Charles Scribners' Sons, 1981), p. 62.

2. The terms "narrative" and "story" will be used interchangeably.

3. Richard Rorty, *Objectivity, Relativism, and Truth* (New York: Cambridge University Press, 1991), p. 21.

4. Daniel Dennett, *Consciousness Explained* (Boston: Little, Brown Publishing Company, 1991), p. 418.

5. Jerome Bruner, *Acts of Meaning* (Cambridge: Harvard University Press, 1990), pp. 99–138.

6. Jerome Bruner, *Actual Minds, Possible Worlds* (Cambridge: Harvard University Press, 1986), p. 13.

7. Joseph Chilton Pearce, "The Risk of Evolution," *Parabola* 17, 2 (1992), 54–60.

8. Alisdair MacIntyre, *After Virtue, 2nd Edition* (Notre Dame: University of Notre Dame Press, 1984), p. 106.

9. Paul Ricoeur, *A Ricoeur Reader: Reflection and Imagination* (Toronto: University of Toronto Press, 1992), pp. 425–26.

10. Bruner, *Acts of Meaning*, p. 111.

11. George Howard, "Cultural Tales: A Narrative Approach to Thinking, Cross-Cultural Psychology, and Psychotherapy," *American Psychologist* 46, 3 (1991), 187–197.

12. Dennett, *Consciousness Explained*, p. 418.

13. Alice Miller, *Thou Shalt Not Be Aware* (New York: Meridan Press, 1986), pp. 1–8.

14. Kieran Egan, *Teaching as Storytelling* (Chicago: University of Chicago Press, 1986), p. 37.

15. James McClendon, *Systematic Theology: Ethics* (Nashville: Abingdon Press, 1986), pp. 17–46.

16. As quoted in James Childress, *Who Should Decide?* (New York: Oxford University Press, 1982), p. 38.

17. Elie Wiesel, article in *Parade Magazine*, 1992.

18. Johann Baptist Metz quoting Theodor Adorno in "A Short Apology of Narrative" in Stanley Hauerwas and L. Gregory Jones, *Why Narrative?* (Grand Rapids: Wm. B. Eerdmans Publishing Company, 1989), pp. 260–61.

19. Robert Coles, *The Call of Stories* (Boston: Houghton Mifflin, 1989), pp. 28–30.

20. As quoted in Stanley Hauerwas, *Naming the Silences* (Grand Rapids: Wm. B. Eerdmans Publishing Company, 1990), pp. 102–112.

21. Arthur Kleinman, *The Illness Narratives* (New York: Basic Books, 1988), p. 50.

22. Richard Katz, *Boiling Energy* (Cambridge: Harvard University Press, 1982), p. 43.

23. Barry Lopez, *Crossing Open Ground* (New York: Vintage Press, 1988), p. 69.

Chapter 21:
Listen, Real Hard This Time, To the Gospel of God

1. Fred Craddock, *Overhearing the Gospel* (Nashville: Abingdon Publishing Company, 1978).

2. Tomie De Paola, *Tomie De Paola's Book of Bible Stories* (New York: Putnam/ Zondervan, 1990).

Chapter 22:
Steve and the Behavior Mod God

1. The other verse that is Steve's favorite is Philippians 4:13: "I can do all things through him who strengthens me." Steve acknowledges that God in Christ gives us the strength to live a Christian life, which means "not trying to do evil things."

2. Walter Brueggemann, *Interpretation Bible Commentary: Genesis* (Atlanta: John Knox Press, 1982), p. 26.

Chapter 23
Randy's Coat of Many Colors

1. Barry Lopez, *Crow and Weasel* (San Francisco: North Point Press, 1991), quote found in the inside jacket cover.

2. Daniel Dennett, *Consciousness Explained* (Boston: Little, Brown Publishing Company, 1991), p. 418.

3. Lavinia Derwent, *Joseph and the Coat of Many Colors* (New York: Scholastic Press, 1965).

Chapter 24
Being a Spiritual Dude:
Lessons from Living with Disabled Adolescents

1. Tourette's syndrome is a neurological disorder characterized by excessive nervous energy and extravagance of strange motions, e.g., involuntary ticks, noises, and grimaces. See Oliver Sacks, *The Man Who Mistook His Wife For a Hat* (New York: Harper & Row, 1987), pp. 92–101.